CIRCUIT DOWN !

How to Solve That Household Electrical Mystery

By Larry Dimock

A guide for U.S. and Canadian
homeowners to solve problems
in their electrical circuits

Circuit Down is a work of non-fiction. The author, publisher, and bookseller make no explicit guarantees as to the accuracy of the information it contains.

First Edition. Published by Lulu.com (I.D. 856638). Also available in spiral-bound edition.

ISBN: 978-1-4303-1307-6

CONTENTS

WHY AND HOW TO USE THIS GUIDE

CHAPTER 1

Purpose. Scope. Safety. Disclaimer.

Purpose and Scope

This guide is a reference for U.S. or Canadian homeowners, for understanding and dealing with problems that occur in their electrical circuits. *Circuit Down* covers the malfunctions that happen in the following places: the power company service line, the main electrical panel, connections and devices along the circuits for lights and outlets, and some of the appliances served.

It is not meant to help with electrical design, installation, upgrading, remodel projects, or even preventive maintenance. There are many resources available for such electrical needs. I will not duplicate their material. What is unique in *Circuit Down* is that it covers all the troublesome things that can happen in a wiring system. The book helps you to identify and locate your particular problem. Quite often you can then do something about it without bringing a professional in.

If you are in the midst of an electrical crisis at home, I want you to be helped right away without having to absorb too many unrelated things. You just need to get your problem taken care of. I suggest you start at whatever chapter seems likely to help. For instance, you might decide to dive into the Diagnostic Tree [80] or the Frequently Answered Questions [92].

On the other hand, you may not be in any need at present. Half the fun of home ownership is learning what makes the house or condo tick. But half the frustration is learning this the hard way: by trial, error, worry, and wasted money. So this guide lets you learn some of it more easily. You can pull it off the shelf for a few evenings to further your do-it-yourself education. Then when a problem shows up, remember that it is on the shelf.

This material was first developed as pages of my electrician business website. The bracketed cross-references are to page numbers. A few matters are missing. Low-voltage, communication, and media wiring are not within its scope. I do not go into the troubleshooting of fluorescent lights or "smart home" (X-10) controls. I do not give much space to solving underground wiring trouble. A line had to be drawn somewhere, at least for this edition.

Overall, the concept of *Circuit Down* is Home Electrical Troubleshooting:

- **Home** includes any residence: a house, condominium, apartment, or mobile home.
- **Electrical** means the alternating-current wiring system of the home.
- **Troubleshooting** here means the process of investigating (and usually fixing) malfunctions after they have appeared.

Your electrical system is not simple to understand, but I find that people are more capable of understanding than they have told themselves or been told.

Safety: I'm Only Going to Say This Once

Some home electrical troubleshooting can be done without the potential of shock to the do-it-yourselfer. Some cannot. In either case, try to understand your electrical system enough to avoid shocks. **Even when you think you have turned off the right things, treat them, if possible, as if they might still be live.** In addition, keep any testers or tools with metal parts from making unintended contact with potentially live or grounded parts, because burns and injuries are possible. Also, in reconnecting or repairing things in your system, the more you attend to proper procedures, the less you risk future disruptions, shocks, or fire hazards.

Disclaimer

The text and diagrams forming this guide, *Circuit Down*, are meant to assist you with general knowledge and advice toward diagnosing and solving electrical malfunctions. They are not complete, may contain minor errors, and may not apply accurately to your specific situation. They are not to be relied on as guidance for installation or for electrical systems that are non-residential or are outside the U.S. and Canada. Personal contact with live electrical parts can result in shock, even fatal shock. Contact of tools with live parts can result in burns or injury in some cases. Miswiring can result in shock hazard, or damage to equipment, appliances, and electronics. Inadequate wiring procedures can lead to unreliability of the system or to the possibility of fire. You, not the author, publisher, or bookseller, are responsible for any such hazards that you encounter or produce if you work on your electrical system. Your legal right to work on some parts of your system may be limited in your state, and permits may be required for some work. Contacting a local electrician to come to your home is always an option and may still be necessary after using this guide.

BACKGROUND

Chapter 2

Your Home Electrical System

Headings in This Chapter

Your Overall System

Electricity flows between the power company and your lights and appliances. Along its path are your panel, its breakers, wires, switches and outlets. There are many connections along these paths that can be disrupted or fail. There are also ways that electricity could go places you don't want it to. Here is a schematic picture of all the major parts of your electrical system:

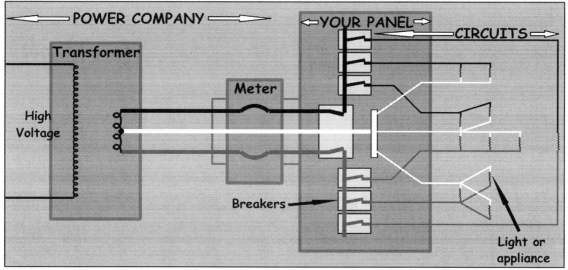

U.S./Canadian 120/240-volt home electrical system schematic. Details are described in the diagrams that follow.

The Power Company

Your electrical utility company and its distribution system bring power over wires and through switches and transformers from the generating plant all the way to a point of connection at your home. The utility's system itself can have trouble, affecting things in your home. Its built-in safety features usually stop power in those cases. However, connections, broken lines, storms, imperfections, or mistakes can sometimes allow unusual voltages into your system, possibly damaging parts of it. The sensitivity of home electronic equipment has made us more aware of this possibility. We commonly use surge protectors to guard against this. But some unusual voltage problems are difficult to protect against. This diagram gives a closer look at the source of 120 and 240 volts in the company's transformer near your home:

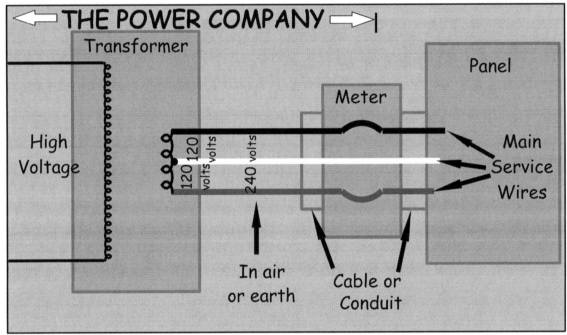

Typical arrangement of service from the electrical utility company

Your Main Panel

Your central *breaker panel* (or *fuse box*) directs electricity through your home as a number of separate *circuits*. **The electricity of a circuit flows between the panel and the electricity "users" along two wires.** In the panel these two wires originate at a double *circuit breaker* or, more often, at a single circuit breaker plus the *neutral bar*. The breaker or fuse will interrupt this flow, the *current* [131], if it ever approaches a level that would overheat the wires' insulation. There may be in the panel a distinct "main" breaker that can shut off power to most or all the circuits. If not, there could be one near the power company's meter. Connections at or in the main breaker or the utility's meter can become unreliable. Being central, this would affect much of the power in your home. If a main breaker were made to trip off, all your power would probably be missing.

Compare a main panel as I have diagrammed it so far with how a typical panel is arranged:

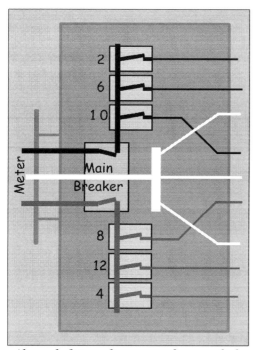 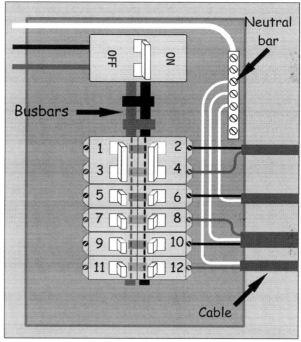

Above left is a diagram of a panel showing, as gray and black, the two "phases" that are each able to provide 120 volts with the white neutral, or 240 volts with each other, to run a circuit. But the picture to the right shows a typical panel more accurately in how the two phases are distributed to the breakers. Notice how, as gray and black, two bus bars alternate down either column of breakers. The right-hand picture shows how wires really leave a panel – in cables. The breakers in the left diagram are numbered according to how they are numbered in the right picture. In both, breakers #2 and #4 make up a 240-volt circuit, as will be seen in the next diagram.

Circuits

A circuit is a path over which electric current can flow around between an electric source and the items run by the electricity. With the circuit in a home, the path is rarely a single loop. If it were, the operation or failure of a circuit would be easier to grasp. But it is not so simple. Most circuits in a home are complex, involving sub-loops. This diagram lets you trace the path of one circuit as it goes through your system:

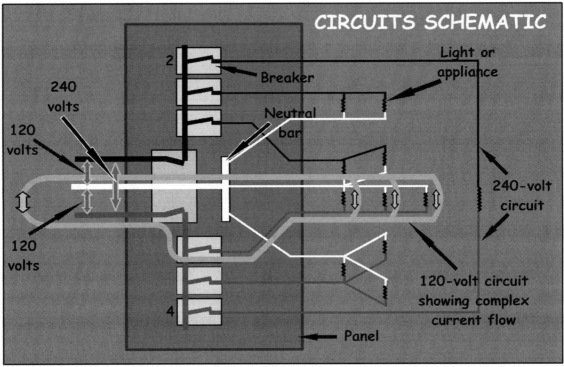

A circuit is able to run items when the path is complete through them (on right) and around to and through the transformer (on left). Direction of flow changes from instant to instant and is called alternating current. Distinguish the arrows showing actual current flow from those merely indicating voltage relationships.

By Code, a dedicated circuit is used for each of most large appliances. Examples would be an electric range, electric water heater, electric dryer, or central air conditioning. These, as well as electric heaters, will have two (joined) breakers in order to use 240 volts rather than the 120 volts used by most other items. A dedicated circuit of 120 volts is usually provided for each dishwasher, disposal, gas or oil furnace, and clothes washer. **Most other 120-volt circuits tend to serve a number (from 2 to 20) of lights and outlets.** There are usually two circuits for the outlets in the kitchen/dining area, and these use a heavier wire capable of 20 amps of current. When we speak of "120" volts, this is an average for general purposes. "120" voltage in a home may actually be about 114 up to about 126 volts. I define voltage at [134].
Circuits serving more than one outlet or light pass power on from one to the next, by means of connections to the device itself or in the box the device is mounted in. So along any one circuit, there are many places where electricity can fail to get through.

These would include the circuit breaker and its connections, connections at devices and boxes, within switches, and the contacts of a receptacle right where you plug something in. Troubleshooting electrical problems in your house will depend on a basic grasp of these matters.

Wires: Hot, Neutral, Ground

To understand the function that different wires in a circuit play, consider first our use of terms. Because a house is provided with alternating current, the terms *positive* and *negative* do not apply as they do to direct current in batteries and cars. Instead, the power company is providing electricity that will flow back and forth 60 times per second. The electricity flows through the transformer, on the one hand, and the operating household items, on the other hand, by way of the continuous wire paths between them.

Two of the transformer's terminals are isolated from the earth and the third is connected to the earth (see bottom diagram below). We call these isolated wires *hot* or *live* because anything even slightly connected to the earth (like us!), when touching a hot wire, provides, along with the earth, an accidental path for electricity to flow between that wire and the transformer's "grounded" terminal.

A circuit's **hot** wire is, we might say, one half of the path the circuit takes between the electrical source and the operating items (*loads*). The other half, in the case of a 120-volt circuit, is the **neutral** wire. For a 240-volt circuit, the other half is a hot wire from the other phase – the other hot coming from the transformer. When they are turned on (operating, running), the loads are part of the path of the current and are where the electricity is doing its intended work.

Hot wires are distributed into your home from a number of circuit breakers or fuses in your panel. They are typically black, occasionally red or even white, and never green or bare. The earth-related neutral wires in your home are also distributed from your panel, but from a (single) neutral bar. Neutral wires are always supposed to be white. Contact with them should not shock you because they are connected to the earth much better than you can be. But contact with a hot, even one that is white-colored, will tend to shock you.

Besides black, red, and white wires, the cables in homes wired since the 1960's also contain a bare or green **ground***(ing)* wire. Like the neutral, it is ultimately connected to the transformer's grounded terminal. But this wire is not connected so as to be part of the normal path of flow around the circuit. Instead, it is there to connect to the metal parts of lights and appliances. This way, a path is provided "to ground" if a hot wire should contact such parts. Otherwise you or I could be the best path, if we touched them. In other words, when a ground wire does carry current, it is taking care of an otherwise dangerous situation. In fact, it usually carries so much current suddenly, that it causes the breaker of the circuit to trip for such a *short*. This alerts us that a problem needs attention.

See if you can follow the different paths taken by normal current and a short-to-ground:

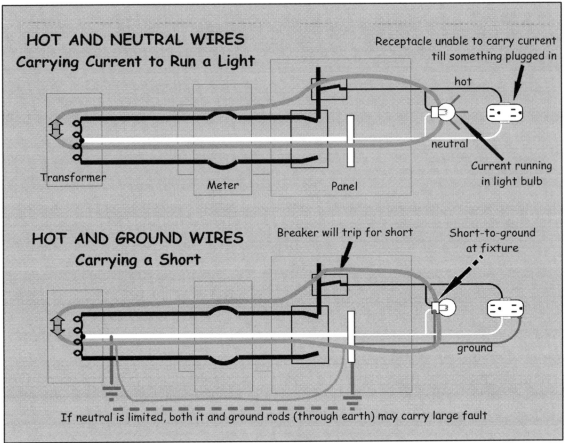

HOT AND NEUTRAL WIRES
Carrying Current to Run a Light

Receptacle unable to carry current
till something plugged in

hot

neutral

Current running
in light bulb

Transformer

Meter

Panel

HOT AND GROUND WIRES
Carrying a Short

Breaker will trip for short

Short-to-ground
at fixture

ground

If neutral is limited, both it and ground rods (through earth) may carry large fault

We intend current to use the white wire (neutral) to complete the circuit normally (top). The extreme current of a short circuit will commonly follow an "emergency path." It can include ground wires, the main neutral, ground rods, and the earth (bottom diagram). In both diagrams the circuit path is indicated roughly by the gray loop.

Switching

By Code, convention, and other good reasons, **only hot wires are supposed to be switched**, never neutrals or grounds. A switch is a device that continues the hotness of a hot wire on through to, say, a light. Or else discontinues that hotness. So the black wire between a switch and its light is not always actually hot. When it is not hot, its black or red color is still valid, to remind us that it will sometimes be hot. See how a household switch works:

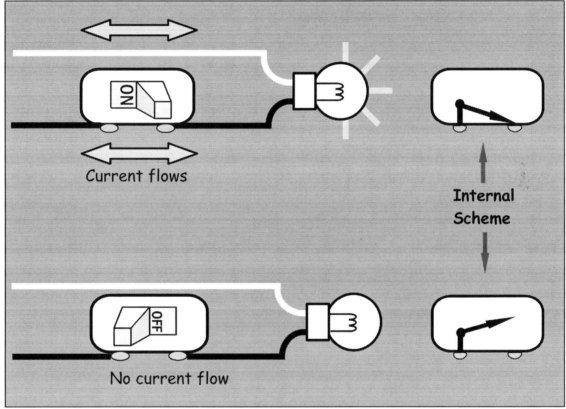

The single-pole (normal on-off) switch. Only a hot wire is affected by a switch, which completes or disrupts the circuit, and current, through the light.

There is a form of switching in which two or more switches can each control a light. These are generally called **three-way switches**. They work by one switch continuing hotness to another, on one or the other of two *traveler* wires that run between the switches. The final switch connects either the hot traveler or the unhot traveler to the light, thus energizing the light or not. I give more discussion and diagrams of 3- and 4-way switches in Chapter 5 [24].

Other specialized switches include dimmers, motion sensors, photocells, timed switches, low-voltage switches, and "smart home" (X-10) switches. You will find tips about these and other devices and appliances in Chapter 21 [104].

CHAPTER 3

How Things Go Wrong

Why should a system which has few moving parts be subject to failures of various kinds? Realize that every technology designs its systems with economy in mind. Even the best available wire connector, for instance, could have been made from even better materials. That would have made problems with it even less likely.

Also, there is such a thing as wear and tear on electrical components. Current flowing through wires and connections creates heat and other stresses that affect the quality of insulating materials and the conductivity of metal surfaces. Add to this the effect of repeated use. Plugging and unplugging appliances at a receptacle gradually loosens its hold on the prongs being plugged in.

Besides these, there is the matter of workmanship. The reliability of the system depends on the care taken to set it up. From the engineer designing a switch to the person installing it, there can be fudging or errors. How tight should a screw be that holds a wire in place? This is something ultimately learned by experience, even though a manufacturer may specify what torque should be applied. Finally, any time your system is reworked even slightly, there is room for error – from ignorance or inattention.

So both the human and the material worlds contribute to the malfunctions this guide is trying to pick up after. The need for troubleshooting is built in.

What are the kinds of things that could possibly go wrong in your electrical system? Consider two ends of the spectrum. At one end, you are familiar with a light bulb burning out. On the other end, you have experienced times when neighborhood power to your home has been interrupted – briefly or for a number hours. Between these, there is quite a variety of other possible trouble points.

To grasp the scope of possible problems, and to lay a groundwork for a strategy to solve them, consider the relation between symptoms and causes. **We can categorize what goes wrong by the symptoms produced or by the cause.** These two aspects are related to some degree, as will be illustrated soon in a chart. First, consider the possible symptoms.

Symptoms Spelled Out

• **Does not work.** Some things don't work. This is the most common trouble.
• **Goes on and off at will or blinks or flickers.** Things are working now but in the past some things have gone out for awhile and later come back on on their own. Or unusual flickering or blinking of lights has been noticed.
• **Runs dim or bright sometimes.** Lately, things often dim down or brighten at will or in response to turning something on or off. This goes on for more than three seconds at a time. This category is to be distinguished from the previous one.
• **Won't go off.** Something won't turn off by means of its switch or other control device.
• **Shocks.** Someone experienced a shock.

Now see the relation of these symptoms to their possible causes:

SYMPTOM →	→	→	→	→
CAUSE ↓	**Does not work**	**Goes off and on at will or flickers**	**Runs dim or bright sometimes**	**Won't go off**	**Shocks**
Short/ Ground-fault/ Overload	Yes	–	–	–	–
Circuit or main wire connection open	Yes	Yes partially	Yes	–	–
Ground-fault with no ground	–	–	–	–	Yes
Miswiring	Yes	–	–	Yes	Yes
Mis-set or bad device	Yes	Yes	–	Yes	–

Causes Spelled Out

1. **Overload/ Short/ Ground-fault.** I group these three causes together because they are ultimate causes behind tripped breakers, blown fuses, or tripped GFCIs (all of which stop electrical items from working). Let's distinguish the three:
   a. An *overload* occurs when in its normal operation a circuit has carried a little too much current a little too long. The wires will be getting too hot, and so the breaker trips off to prevent this. You were running too much on that circuit.
   b. A *short circuit*, or short, is an unintended connection from a hot wire "to ground"

by way of the neutral wire or (less technically) by way of the ground wire or anything else providing a good path to the earth. A short will usually trip a breaker because the flow of current is huge, not being limited and safe by design, as it is when running lights and appliances. Current still flows around between the hot and the grounded points of origin, and so it is still technically going in a "circuit." The rare 240-volt short would be between two "opposite" hot wires.

   c. A particular "short" (in the broad sense) is the *ground-fault*. It involves contact from a hot wire to something grounded other than the neutral itself – as in the diagram at [12]. If there is, ahead of the fault, a ground-fault circuit interrupter (GFCI) outlet [31] or GFCI breaker, it will sense this and trip power off. Even when a ground-fault is not strong enough to trip a normal breaker, it is a "leaking" of current off of the intended path and therefore a possible shock hazard.

2. **Circuit or main wire connection open.** An *open* refers to an unintended discontinuity somewhere along a circuit's path. It may be a break, a gap, or a deterioration. Typically, a wire has become too loose at a point where it is supposed to pass current on to another wire. See all the places that can develop an open:

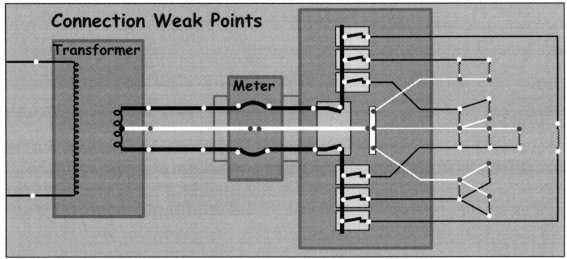

Points of connection, shown above as dots, can be where an open happens in the circuit or the system. In addition, any breakers, switches, or other devices can have vulnerable connections or can disrupt part of a circuit's path by an internal (device) problem. When these weak points in the system fail, they will affect all the circuits or items of a circuit that depend on them for completing the path needed for operation.

To see what bad connections sometimes look like go to the photo at [119]. Here is a closer look at what is behind some bad connections:

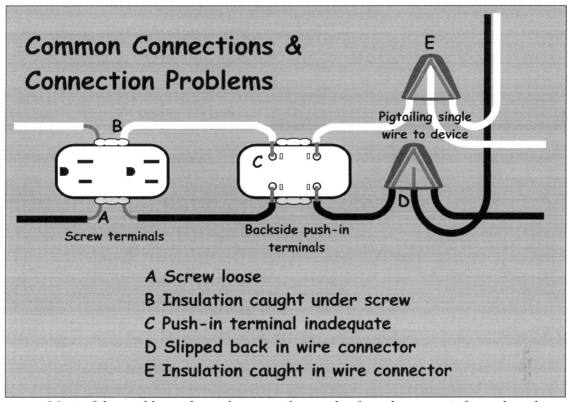

Common Connections &
Connection Problems

E

Pigtailing single
wire to device

B

C

A

D

Screw terminals

Backside push-in
terminals

A Screw loose
B Insulation caught under screw
C Push-in terminal inadequate
D Slipped back in wire connector
E Insulation caught in wire connector

*Most of the problems shown here are the result of careless or uninformed work.
"Good enough" must always be said at some point by the best workmen, but it is not a
motto.*

An open at a main wire – at the panel, meter, or line from the power company – will disable more than one branch circuit. In addition, it can affect several circuits with a weird dimming or brightening effect [38]. The combined 120- and 240-volt system provided to U.S. and Canadian homes is behind this. A similar effect can appear in the case of an open neutral of a two-circuit cable [36].

3. **Ground-fault with no ground.** Shocks happen when a person's body provides the unintended path between a hot (faulting) device, fixture, or appliance and a grounded wire, device, fixture, appliance, pipe, or the earth itself. Whatever should have grounded the hot item is either missing or out of contact – is open. Otherwise the situation would have tripped a breaker or GFCI.

4. **Miswiring.** Poor workmanship can result in the other cause-categories, but this category refers to actual mistakes made in connections, often when a device is replaced.

5. **Mis-set or bad device.** Switches, outlets, light fixtures, and light bulbs can fail to operate as they should because of breakage, arcing, heat, internal wear, damage, corrosion, or manual settings on them that have been changed. This cause will tend to affect only the thing itself or, in the case of switching devices, the things meant to be controlled by it.

CHAPTER 4

Diagram of a Typical Circuit

Tour of a Circuit

At the end of this chapter, you will find two diagrams [21][23] of a typical U.S. or Canadian household circuit. The first is explained in the paragraphs that follow here; it shows examples of connections in electrical boxes and at the devices mounted in them. The second diagram is not explained separately and portrays a floorplan of where this same circuit might have been run in some rooms of a house. In the diagrams you may recognize the wiring of the outlets, switches, and lights in your own home. A description of the first diagram follows now.

The boxes are shown as light-gray areas. The dark gray background represents the area between boxes – usually inaccessible – where the cables containing the wires run in the ceiling, wall, and floor framing of the home. As you can see, between any two boxes, either two or three wires run, corresponding to two or three-conductor cable. For a GFCI wiring diagram see [31].

Ground wires (bare or green wires) are not shown. Red wires are shown as gray. Connections are shown either as wires making contact with the side-screw terminals of devices or as wires bundled into wire connectors. The diagram is not meant as a guide for doing wiring. For example, the white wires connected to some switches here should nowadays be taped red or black, so they are not mistaken for neutrals. The diagram is more to familiarize you with what you may encounter in an existing home.

This circuit starts with A4 receiving hot (black) and neutral (white) wires from the main electrical panel. Imagine the panel to the left. A4 passes hots and neutrals to nearby receptacles A3 and A5 by means of their wires' contact with the terminals on A4. Side-screws are shown here, but another place to terminate is in holes on the back side. A3 and A5 are the beginnings of the two primary branches of this circuit, and we can identify several sub-branches that are developed beyond them.

Looking ahead, A3 will feed a string of boxes one direction (A2, B2, A1, B1, C2) and another string through B3, B4, C3, D3, D2, D1, and C1. Meanwhile the branch at A5 provides connection out to B5, C5, D5, D4, and C4. It also sends power through A6 to

B6, C6, and D6. A6 also sends power out to A7, B7, C7, and D7.

Let's follow the sub-branch that goes up from A3. A3 needs to get its hot and neutral connections passed on so that two lights (A1 and B1) can burn – not all the time, but according to what the switches at A2, B2, and C2 say. A2 is a normal single-pole switch, as seen by its two side-screws. According to the position of its handle, it will either let its light (A1) get the hot connection or not; the neutral connection at A2 (a wire connector) is not affected by the switch.

Meanwhile, however, A2's box needs to help the switches at B2 and C2 receive power so they can run their light (B1). These two switches (B2 and C2) are three-way switches [24], as seen by their three side-screws. If either of their handles moves, it changes the hot's connectedness to the light. This particular set of 3-way switches is set up in this way: B2's switch sends hotness to C2's along either the gray or the white (called *travelers*) according to which traveler terminal B2's switch internally passes its hotness on to, from the black terminal. Similarly, the black at C2 will be made hot or not, depending on which traveler terminal the switch internally connects it to. This black wire (the *light leg*) is the one whose hotness or unhotness will let the light burn or not; so back at B2's box it must be bundled with the black that goes to B1, where the light is.

Let's go back now to the other sub-branch that goes out from A3. It will run a light (B3) and three receptacles (D1, D2, and D3). The light will be controlled by switch B4, D2 and D3 by switch C3, and D1 by switch C1 (switched receptacles!). Here's how. A3 feeds power to the B3 box, where the light gets its neutral connection immediately. But the light's hotness will depend on switch B4 (once B4 has received constant hotness from B3 by a wire connector at B3). That wire connector at B3 also sends hotness on to the rest of this sub-circuit on the black going to C3. Don't rush on. Yes, a white wire is being used as a hot down to B4; that's the way a cable of two wires comes – black and white. Nowadays this white should be painted or taped black or red when installed.

Now, C3 has received its hot, and the neutral bundle at B3 has also given C3 its neutral. C3's switch is mainly going to switch the left half of the receptacles at D2 and D3. So the neutral simply ties through in C3's box to reach D3, D2, and D1. But the hot at C3 must also tie through (besides giving hotness to one end of the C3 switch) in order for the right half of these receptacles to be able to run things plugged into them all the time, regardless of what any switches are doing to the left side. The two halves of these receptacles have to be isolated from each other (on the hot side only!) by breaking off the metal tabs that normally join the halves electrically. Compare the look of the hot-side screws in D3, D2, and D1 with the other receptacles on the page.

The gray wire from C3 to D3 is hot or not, according to switch C3. This switchedness is passed on to D2's left side, as also D3's constant hot is passed on to the right side of D2.

D1's left side is controlled by a different switch – at C1. D1 has received neutral and constant hot from D2. Now for C1 to switch D2's left side, the white wire from D1 to C1 must take hotness to C1. Then the C1 switch can send hotness or deadness back to D1's left side. The hot-side terminal tab of D1 must be broken away to prevent the left side from being hot all the time (unswitchable).

We're over half-way through! Next see how A5 sends power out to run lights B5 and D5. A5's neutral goes to connect directly to B5's light. For this neutral to also reach light D5, it must first go the same path as the other wires in its cable, to C5. Those other wires, gray and black, want to relate light B5 to switch C5 and also want to pass a constant hot on to the switches (C4 and D4), that will end up switching D5. So the neutral from B5 ties through box C5 to give D5 its neutral connection. No switched light (like B5 or D5) personally needs a constant hot in its box, but since it was convenient for the cable guy to run A5's power toward D5 by way of box B5, the hot ties through at B5 and at a terminal on C5's switch and at D5 itself. This sets up hotness to run on a white to and through the 3-way switches, C4 and D4, with D4 finally determining the hotness of the black that goes to the light D5. Back at B5, hotness for the light comes back (or not) from switch C5 on the gray.

Let's continue on another sub-branch. A6 receives good hot and neutral paths from A5. A6 will power our last two sub-branches of the whole circuit. First is the line from A6 through B6 and C6 to D6. This scenario is similar to the one just described for A5 sending power through light and switch boxes B5 and C5. In this case, however, power from A6 reaches the switch box first, rather than the light box. Comparing the diagrams of the two switch boxes and the two light boxes, they are identical. The difference, we could say, is that now the gray wire switching light C6 is "going" in the same direction as the other wires that extend power further out on the circuit; whereas the gray for light B5 "came back from" switch C5. This (row 6) sub-branch ends with receptacle D6 receiving power, with no one to send it on to, except of course to whatever is plugged into it.

The last section of the circuit involves A6 sending power down to a 3-way switching scheme [27] that has yet another look. A7 and B7 tie the neutral through their boxes for lights C7 and D7 to use. The hot at A7 connects to the non-traveler terminal (called the *common*), and its hotness is passed by the switch onto either the black or gray. Inside switch B7 one of these travelers is in contact with B7's common, so that the black from B7 to the lights will be hot or not. Finally, light C7, besides attaching to the incoming black and white itself, is involved by its wire connectors in passing this same switched power on to its friend D7.

Two Troubleshooting Puzzles For This Circuit

1. **Beginner.** The circuit in the diagram was working fine, until one day nothing in rows 1, 2, or 3 worked anymore. A tester registered no hotness in these three rows at any of the terminals, wire connectors, or bare-copper ends of the wires themselves. But everything in rows 4 through 7 still worked, other than B4 of course. Testing was not done on the working rows. I will tell you that there is a poor connection or contact somewhere. Exactly where is it?
2. **Intermediate.** The beginner solved the problem above, but a year later something else went wrong. Maybe a beginner made all the connections in this circuit. This time light D5 stopped working. Everything else still worked. No, the bulb was fine. And testing revealed that hotness was getting everywhere it should and that all the switches were doing their jobs. Which connection is bad, or if there is more than one possible place, how many and where?

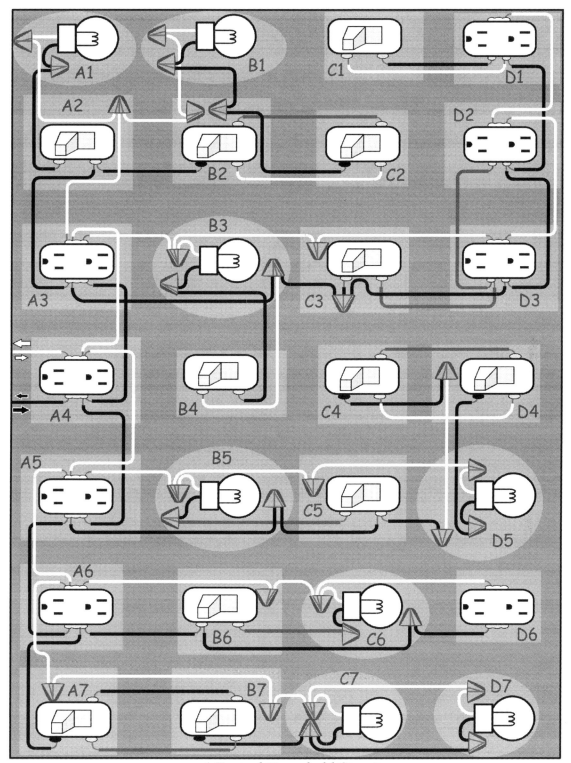

A Typical Household Circuit

PUZZLE ANSWERS:

1. The bad connection has to be where the black wire from A4 to A3 is connecting to A4. That is what would account for no hotness registering anywhere in rows 1-3. If the bad spot were at the A3 end of the same wire, that end of the wire would itself show hotness, even though the screw it was supposed to connect to would not.

2. If hotness was getting everywhere, the bad connection must be a bad neutral (white). Since everything worked before D5 on the circuit, the bad neutral could only be at three possible points: a.) At D5's own wire connector for whites; b.) At the white-wire connector in C5, which wouldn't bother that switch's operation; or c.) At the white-wire connector at B5. The light at B5 could itself have a good white connection, but the white that goes from B5 to C5 might not.

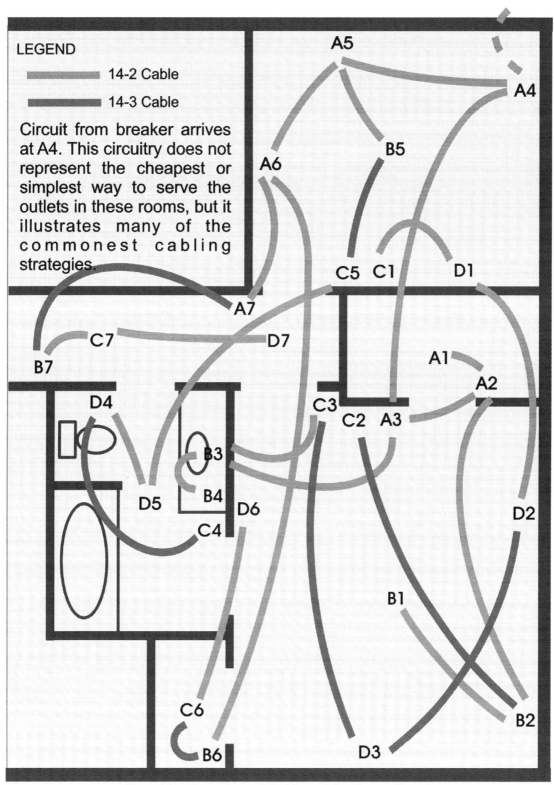

LEGEND

14-2 Cable

14-3 Cable

Circuit from breaker arrives at A4. This circuitry does not represent the cheapest or simplest way to serve the outlets in these rooms, but it illustrates many of the commonest cabling strategies.

Possible Floorplan of Cables of the Same Circuit

CHAPTER 5

Three and Four-Way Switches

How complicated can 3-way switches be? Consider this: since a 2-switch system has 3 wires to be connected to 3 terminals at each box, it works out that only 4 out of 36 possibilities will work. Each 4-way switch in-between would worsen the odds by a factor of 3, and any defective switch or connection further complicates things. What is going to be easier – trial and error or understanding the 3-way switch system?

Headings in this chapter

Terminology and How a 3-Way System Works
Generic 3-Way and 4-Way Diagrams
Wire Colors in a 3- or 4-Way Switch System
The Basic 3-Way Switch Arrangement
3-Way Switch Variations
The Basic 4-Way Switch Arrangement
4-Way Switch Variations
Troubleshooting 3- and 4-Way Switches

Terminology and How a 3-Way System Works

Multiple switches may be located at several approaches to a room in order to turn the room's lights on or off from any one of those locations. They do this by sending or stopping hotness from traveling along two alternative paths – wires called **travelers**. Hotness enters into the system at one **three-way** type switch, which we will call the **hot end**. According to the position of its handle, hotness travels on to the next switch on one of the two traveler wires. If this next switch is the only other switch, it is also of the 3-way type and can be called the **leg end**. It will pass the hotness on to the light(s), but only if its handle happens to be in the position that is in contact with the particular traveler that is bringing the hotness. If there were any more switches between these two (electrically), they would simply pass hotness along. But they would be able to change which traveler wire the hotness continues on. To do this, these (third, fourth, etc.) switches must be **four-way** type switches – a different animal than the first and last switches in the electrical line. Four-way switches have four terminals to connect two traveler pairs to. Three-way switches have three terminals, with the one that is not for the two travelers being called the **common**. At the hot end, the incoming hot wire is connected to the common terminal. At the leg end, the wire attached to the common is the one that goes to the light(s). This will all be made clear in the diagrams that follow.

The British perhaps use more common sense in naming these "2-way switches," but in North America we are stuck with "3-way." I think I've noticed some Canadians and others talking about "tree-way switches." Anyway, I refer to these switches, wires, and the lights they control as a 3-way "system" not a 3-way "circuit," because that can be confused with the branch-circuit and breaker that such a system is part of.

Generic 3-Way and 4-Way Diagrams

If you need to review what a circuit is or the function of a neutral wire, see [10]. Here you see a diagram of the layout of 3-way switch wiring and what goes on inside the switches:

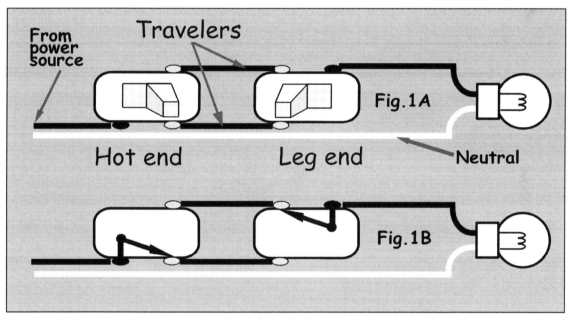

3-way Switches. *Figure 1A shows hot and neutral entering from left. Since a neutral is not switched, switching of the hot will determine whether the circuit to run the light will be completed or not. Fig. 1B shows what is going on inside these same switches. You can see that there is no path for the hot to get through. The switch mechanism can pivot the "arrow" over to the other light-colored terminal. Notice that flipping either switch will let hotness through.*

In your mind, play with pivoting the contacts differently and notice that either switch is able to override what the other one did last. Between each switch box and the next, the travelers will be contained in the same cable with each other. At most switch boxes there will be other wires serving other purposes – one or two other wires in the travelers' cable itself and wires in other cables. Usually, but not always, the cable carrying the travelers has another insulated wire, which may be a neutral, a hot, or the leg wire (to the light).

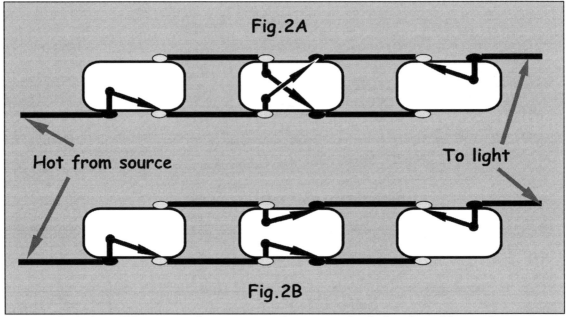

4-way Switches. When more than two switches control a light, the additional ones must have four terminals. Their mechanism must relate the incoming traveler-pair to the outgoing pair in the two ways shown in Fig. 2A&2B – crossed or straight through. Fig. 2A would complete the path to the light. In Fig. 2B the path would be disrupted.

Occasionally a traveler cable will make its way to the next switch by running through the light box itself. The possibly strange routes these cables take and the various functions the non-traveler wires play does not change anything I have said here or will say. **In simplest terms, every normal 3-way system needs** a neutral at the light box, a constant hot at one switch box, travelers between it and the final switch box (passing through any 4-way switches on the way), and a switched leg going from that final box to the light box. How this is all arranged in practice can vary greatly.

There are two abnormal and rare 3-way systems that might be encountered. They are called by various names – California, Hollywood, coast, farmer's, French, Chicago, Carter, lazy Susan, lazy neutral. The names are confused between the two kinds. One is illegal and presents possible shock danger. The other (British, I think) seems allowed by Code and is so different in its concept that few electricians here would even recognize it. What I have to say about 3-way systems is not meant to apply to these systems.

Wire Colors in a 3- or 4-Way Switch System

I will try to describe here what color the insulation on the wires of multiple-switch systems will commonly be, if they are not miswired. Lately, Code is wanting any "factory" whites serving as travelers or as the hot-end hot to be re-marked black or red. Here I am only telling what you will commonly find in most homes. The hot wire at the common terminal of the hot-end switch will be black or, rarely, red or white. The light-leg wire at the common terminal of the leg-end switch will be black or (rarely) red. Each traveler pair is contained in one cable, and will be either black and white or black and red, or red and white. Most other white wires present in these switch boxes are neutrals that are connected to each other and not to any of the switch terminals. Any bare or green wires are grounding wires connected to each other. If the switch has an additional green screw, to meet Code a bare piece should be run to it from all the grounds. To see several ways that 3-way systems are wired, including likely wire colors, see below.

Varieties of 3-way and 4-way Switch Wiring. Since there is a wide variety of ways that 3- and 4-way switches in practice have their cables run and wires connected, I have created a number of examples below to illustrate them, so that you can perhaps recognize your own version.

The Basic 3-Way Switch Arrangement

As I also describe at the generic diagram at [25], normally encountered 3-way systems all share one scheme-theme:

$$— S == S — O$$

where the "S"s are the switches, the "O" is the light, and the lines shown are wires carrying constant (the line on the left) or switchable (the rest) hotness. The neutrals, not being involved in the switching operation, are not shown yet. They can be in the picture in a variety of ways. Nor are boxes or cables containing the wires shown yet; nor any additional lights switched with the one shown; nor any 4-way switches [28].

Here now are two ways you might see this scheme in the flesh, complete with neutrals, boxes, and cables:

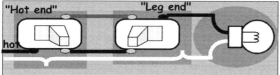 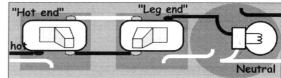

3-Way Switch Variations

There are several common variations on this basic theme, which may look like deviations from it but are not. The main difference is that the following examples all have some of the switch-related wires spliced through boxes on their way to actually connecting to the light or switches. The wire colors shown in the following switch diagrams [28] are not the only ones possible. They are some of what you may encounter, not necessarily how it should be done to current Code. These wiring schemes are often given names, but the names are not consistent.

A. Here the hot arrives at one switch box. It can then be connected through to the other switch to be its hot-all-the-time common, or instead it can attach as common of the switch where it arrived to begin with. Either way, the travelers between the switches end up giving hotness or unhotness to the light "leg." This leg either comes directly off the common of the switch nearest (electrically) to the light, or is tied through to the light from the switch furthest from it. This arrangement is a common one:

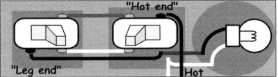

B. Here the hot for the system arrives at the light box, but its functional connection is at whichever switch it is connected through to. The other switch ends up sending the decision of the travelers back by way of the same cable that brought hotness down from the light box:

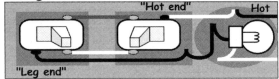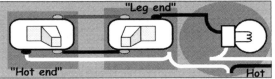

C. Here the travelers from one switch to the other are simply routed through the light box, where connectors pass them on through:

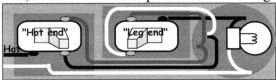

The three variations above (A, B, C) come about from several factors:
- The fact that house-cable comes with either two or three insulated conductors
- The physical relation (direction, order, distance) among the switches and lights
- The available sizes of electrical boxes to hold the wires, lights, and switches
- The direction from which the circuit is approaching the area
- The Code restrictions on how the cabling can be done
- The electrician's preferred tradition

The Basic 4-Way Switch Arrangement

Normally encountered 4-way switch systems all share this scheme-theme:

$$- S = S = S - O$$

where the "S"s, the "O," and the lines are as described at "The Basic 3-way Switch Arrangement" [27]. Here then are two ways you might see this basic scheme, complete with neutrals, boxes, and cables:

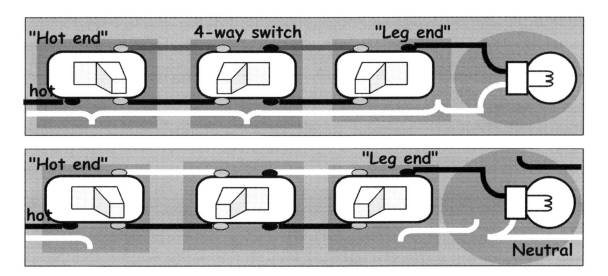

4-Way Switch Variations

As you can see, the picture above corresponds to the diagram for the basic 3-way switch system [27] . Many variations of this basic theme are possible. For instance, each of the 3-way switch schemes (A, B, and C at [28]) will allow a 4-way switch and box to be interposed between the 3-way switch boxes. Then all three switches will work the light(s). Remember, one 3-way switch needs a constant hot, the other needs to "heat up" a wire to the light, a neutral needs to reach the light, and two travelers need to be passed between each switch in succession. Without taking up too much space, here are a few 4-way schemes in very simplified form, inspired by A, B, and C above:

— S == S == S
  |
  O

— O == S == S == S

— S == S == O == S

— S == O == S == S

— O == S == S
  |||
  S

Next, as an example of more possibilities, I show a 4-way system in which the hot cable enters at the 4-way switch's box:

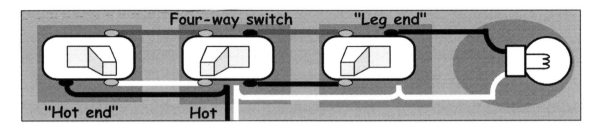

If you have begun to grasp the idea of 4-ways, you may be getting the impression that a person could invent their own way to wire a 3-way or 4-way system. It is true. Whatever works, is not against Code, and is safe is possible. This guide is not to advise you about design, Code, or installation.

Troubleshooting 3- and 4-Way Switches; What Commonly Causes a Malfunction

One of the switches itself can fail. Or the connection of a wire at one of the switches can become loose. Both of these problems can be checked without disconnecting anything. With one prong of a neon tester in your hand, touch the other prong to the common terminal of each three-way switch in turn. If one of those lights it up (is hot) regardless of all possible switch-positions of both switches, that is the hot end. Then just follow whether the next switch (even if it is a 4-way) is passing this hotness on through as expected, based on the diagrams above. Wherever it does not pass through is the bad connection or bad switch.

Someone replacing a switch can do so incorrectly or can install a switch that only has two (non-green) terminals. Replacing a toggle-handle style switch with a large decorator style "rocker" switch can also invite a problem. The location of the terminals on the rocker is quite different. Here the foolproof way to connect is to have the travelers attach to the two same-color screws, and use the remaining common screw for the other wire.

Remember three things:
  • The two travelers are in the same cable with each other.
  • Any pair of switch screws that are the same color as each other are for a traveler pair. One manufacturer shipped one of their 4 way switch models with wrong instructions!
  • The only wire in a 3- and/or 4-way system that is hot all the time when all the switches of the system are disconnected from their wires, is the hot. It will attach to the common terminal of the "hot end" switch.

If you have removed old switches but lost track of the wires' original connections to those switches, I think the troubleshooting tips above should be enough for you to make things right. But if someone has undone other wires besides those that had been attached to the switches, see all the Chapter 5 diagrams and the Typical Circuit [18].

CHAPTER 6

GFCI Outlets

There are often special looking electrical receptacles in bathrooms or kitchens that have "Test" and "Reset" buttons – often black and red – on them. These are ground-fault circuit interrupters – **GFCIs** or **GFIs**. Their purpose is to protect people from electrocution. They do not prevent shock altogether, only deadly shock. And they do not prevent overloads on the circuit. That is the job of a circuit breaker at the main panel.

In the U.S., and in some respects in Canada, GFCIs have been required since 1973 to protect more and more locations in new homes. **See the location details at [71].** This does not mean that each location requiring such protection has to have its own GFCI device. One device will usually be protecting several normal-looking outlets downstream from it. So if outlets have gone dead in bathrooms, kitchen, dining room, garage, laundry, or outdoors, there is a very good chance that a GFCI somewhere has tripped off.

Understand that 99% of the time GFCIs save us by not letting us have their electricity in the first place. Long before you are about to use a protected appliance or light, the GFCI will have sensed most faults and cut power off.

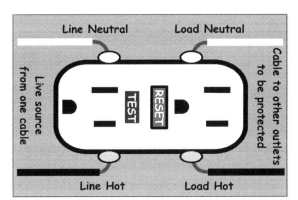 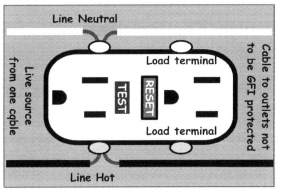

GFCI connections. The GFCI to the left is hooked up so as to sense and protect other outlets. The one to the right is connected so as to pass normal power (no GFCI protection) on to other outlets.

It is also common for a GFCI outlet – or GFCI circuit breaker in the panel – to trip for conditions that might not put you in any danger. This is because the device can't tell the difference between a human body and a wire or a pipe or water. A GFCI is very sensitive to small "leaks" of current, even harmless ones, off of the intended circuit. Often the tripped GFCI will allow itself to be reset, since the cause of its tripping was a passing thing.

One of the silly ways a GFCI outlet will trip is by a person accidentally pressing the test button. This may be a visiting child, or it may be that when someone is unplugging something from the GFCI, their thumb happens to press on the test button.

It is unrealistic for a homeowner to be expected to know where all the GFCIs are in a home, or to know which other normal outlets will be dead from the tripping of a given GFCI outlet. Still, if you have an outage of the receptacles in one of the rooms mentioned above, it may help to look for GFCI outlets in all of those areas and to reset them all. The reset button will need a forceful push. Avoid the test button.

The search to find all possible GFCIs needs to be persistent and thorough. It may be that the bathroom and outdoor outlets are dead from a GFCI in the garage that is never used itself, because it is behind a pile of storage boxes. Or a set of kitchen outlets has gone out because of the GFCI hiding behind the heavy hutch in the dining room or nook.

On most GFCIs is a statement to "Test Monthly." That means pushing the test button, seeing that the reset has popped out, seeing that nothing will run using the outlet at that point, and then pushing the reset. The point of this is to see if the device is still sensing properly, so as to do its job of stopping electrocutions. GFCIs don't have a high rate of failure in regard to sensing ground-faults. When they do fail in this sense, they will still run things, such as a hair dryer. Recent GFCI design requirements seem to be making the test button unnecessary: new GFCIs must fail to deliver power if the GFCI becomes incapable of reacting properly to faults.

Of course, they can fail in other ways, as when they *won't* run things. But be careful not to assume the GFCI is at fault. There could easily be an "open" upstream from it. If someone added your now-dead GFCI unnecessarily when upgrading, the more original GFCI may have tripped somewhere ahead of this one. Above all, don't think the GFCI is defective when it keeps tripping or will not let itself be reset. I have come across only one possible case of defective tripping. GFCIs trip for reasons, including misconnections and an incompatibility with some motors, treadmills, UPSs, dimmers, and fluorescent lights. But more commonly it is for various faults downstream in wiring or plugged-in appliances – both dangerous and harmless faults.

If you are confused about the terms GFCI or GFI, I have comments. Those names are interchangeable, but I reveal my preference in the Glossary [131]. We have some other confusions also. One is whether either term refers to a receptacle-type or to a circuit-breaker-type interrupter. In fact, people are commonly calling either type a "GFCI breaker" or a "GFCI switch." Though they both can have the effect of a switch, that is not their purpose and I discourage that way of talking. As for "breaker," the circuit-breaker-type GFCI does do double-duty as a normal circuit breaker and looks like a breaker and lives in a panel. So it deserves the name "GFCI breaker." Likewise, a receptacle-type GFCI does double-duty as an outlet. Even though it automatically "breaks" part of a circuit when it trips off, to call it a breaker will confuse anyone who is aware that there is a different device by that name already. So we should call this more common device a "GFCI outlet" or a "GFCI receptacle."

Another confusing phrase I hear is "GFCI circuit." Where a true GFCI circuit breaker is used, everything it feeds would certainly be a GFCI-protected branch circuit. Where an outlet-type GFCI is used, the branch circuit it is on always includes something – some wire, at least – that is not being protected or shut off by the device. People want to use the word "circuit" to refer to the items that go dead when the GFCI trips. This is understandable, but "circuit" is not the right word. We need to keep using "circuit" to talk about the whole circuit this outlet and its loads are part of. "Load" [132] is the accepted term for the things being protected.

I don't intend this guide for giving advice on installation, but many **people putting in a combination GFCI-switch device** (GFCI outlet plus switch) seem to need help. One of the wires that comes from the switch part attaches to the (black) wire going to the item to be switched. How you hook the other wire up depends on whether the item to be switched is to be on the same circuit as the receptacle. If it is not, keep it and its neutral totally separate from the GFCI wiring. If the switched item is going to be on the same circuit, then how you proceed depends on whether the switched item should be GFCI-protected or not. If protected, its switch's remaining black would attach somehow to the Load hot terminal. If unprotected, to the Line hot terminal. The switched item's neutral should attach to the corresponding neutral terminal: Load or Line.

CHAPTER 7

Two-Circuit Cables

A particular kind of circuitry often found in U.S. and Canadian homes mirrors the main wiring feeding the home from the power company. It is called a multiwire branch circuit. For our purposes it would be clearer to call it a two-circuit cable. **It involves two hot wires sharing one neutral as their "return" path.** The hot wires are 240 volts apart from each other and each is 120 volts from the neutral. This sort of arrangement saves a little wire at installation time by using a cable containing black, red, and white wires between the panel and (usually just) the first outlet or switch box it is run to.

The two parts of this multi-circuit usually split apart from each other at that point and then behave like most other 120-volt circuits. But if you were to trace the flow of two-circuit current from the panel to that first box at a time when each part of the multicircuit was using different amounts of electricity, here is what you would find:

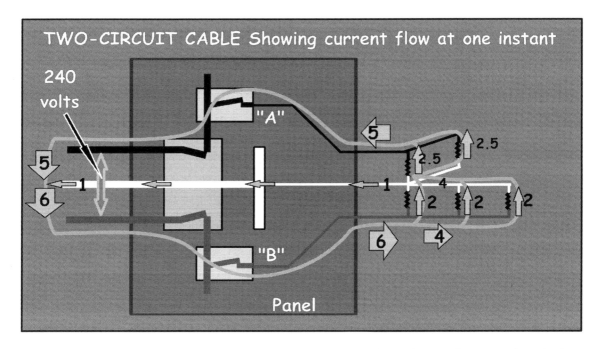

TWO-CIRCUIT CABLE Showing current flow at one instant

If 5 amps is flowing on hot wire A and 6 amps on hot wire B, the neutral path they share will not be found to be carrying 11 amps. That would only happen if the two hots were, against Code, fed from the same main wire through the same bus bar. Instead, only 1 amp would be flowing on the neutral. At a given instant – remember this is alternating current – that one amp would be flowing in the direction that would seem to complete the motion of current in wire B, and against the direction that would seem needed to complete wire A's circuit. Where is A's 5 amps of current "coming from" or "going to" at that instant? It is not connecting to the panel by way of the neutral. It is by way of wire B, driven by the 240 volts between them. Even wire B is sending 5 of its amps along wire A, with the 1 amp difference – the imbalance – going on the neutral. A's 5 amps and 5 of B's 6 amps are the same thing. They are essentially a 240-volt circuit, flowing from breaker to breaker and ultimately out to the two ends of the power company transformer's coil. The whole system for the home is doing this all the time because the two hot main power company wires share one neutral from the panel back to the transformer.

Two-Circuit Open Neutral

There is a disturbing malfunction that can occur with a multi-circuit cable at the panel or a box it goes to. If the neutral connection at the panel's neutral bar or at the box the cable is run to goes bad, the two circuits will become entirely one 240-volt circuit, with one (former) circuit's set of loads arranged in series with the other's.

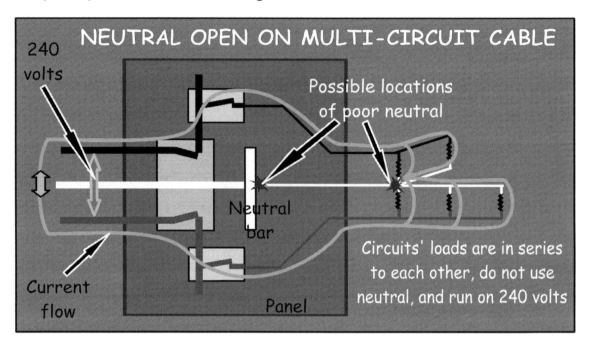

Since their lights and appliances were not designed with such a voltage and connection scheme in mind, the result is that the items served by one former circuit will tend to run brighter than usual and those of the other dimmer. Damage can occur, especially to sensitive electronic equipment. If you notice a sustained **weird dimming of lights in one part of the home and lights burning brighter than normal in another part**, this is one possible cause. The other is a similar situation occurring to the home's whole system when the main neutral [38] is bad.

Two-Circuit Outlets

The kitchen/dining/family room areas of U.S. homes wired in the 1960s and 1970s sometimes had two distinct 20-amp "appliance" circuits reaching each normal (duplex) receptacle by way of one two-circuit cable. Canada's version has been to require single-circuit 20-amp and/or two-circuit 15-amp receptacles at specified kitchen locations. **The hot-side metal tab of a two-circuit receptacle was broken off to isolate top and bottom halves from each other** so that both circuits could be available at one duplex receptacle. The idea was to distribute heavy loads more easily between the two required circuits. The fact that homeowners and home-dwellers were unaware of this made the idea almost useless, in my opinion.

Anyway, by now this well-meaning idea has even backfired. Homeowners or handymen now often replace even just one of these worn or unfashionable receptacles without breaking away the new metal tab on the hot side. What happens then? The two circuits, which were purposely fed from opposite main bus bars to let them share one neutral without overloading it, will pass a 240-volt short between them. If the breaker handles of the two circuits are tied together, as would be required by now, they will both trip, and someone will have to figure out what was done wrong. More often, the breakers are quite separate and the first one to trip thereby prevents the second from tripping. **This actually leaves all the outlets still working.** Why? Because the circuit that didn't trip now feeds its hotness through the unremoved metal tab to the other half of all the outlets. This means that the whole kitchen will now have only one circuit's capacity, instead of two. I have seen homes where one of these breakers has apparently been sitting tripped for years, with people wondering why they can't run more than two appliances at once in their kitchen before the one turned-on breaker trips from an overload.

CHAPTER 8

Open Main Wire – Strange Effects

For a discussion of an open neutral along a single circuit, see [58]. For the effects of an open neutral on two circuits that share a neutral, go to [36]. To compare the abnormal conditions shown below with diagrams of normality, see Chapter 2 [6].

Open Main Neutral

When the main neutral becomes open at some place (explosion, at left in diagram), the ground rods will try to give an alternate path for 120-volt circuits through the earth, but inadequately. So to a large degree the system of circuits is subject to 240 volts. Depending on what is turned on out on the circuits, **240 volts tries to run things by using the neutral bar as a path between its two hot main wires.** Although 240 volts is more powerful, the resistances it goes through in one of its sides (black, for instance) are in series with the ones it goes through in the other (gray). The common result is that some lights in the home will burn dimmer than usual and others brighter. This can be affected by other things in the home turning on or off. Bulbs can blow out and electronics can be damaged.

If the five resistances shown in the left diagram are 60 watt bulbs, they normally each burn at a 60-watt level and use 300 watts together. But with the neutral disabled, they will tend to use only 288 watts, 173 being used by the two black-circuit bulbs burning brightly (about 86 watts each) and 115 watts being used by the three gray-circuit bulbs burning dimly (about 38 watts each). 240-volt items will operate normally.

Open Main Hot

Whenever a main hot becomes open somewhere (explosion, at right in diagram), the system of circuits is effectively disabled in all its 240-volt circuits and in half its 120-volt circuits – the dark gray-wire ones in the diagram. However, **these disabled circuits can conspire to run themselves weakly, using the good main hot** (black) as follows. Any

240-volt circuit that is ready to run (is "on") will take advantage of its connection with both good and bad hots, and of the fact that bad-hot 120-volt circuits have a neutral connection. In the right diagram, good black hotness will find its way through the 4500-watt water heater and from there through its gray-wire breaker and a gray-wire lighting (120-volt) breaker and its three bulbs, to good neutral. The 120-volt-powered current going on this strange path will run the water heater at 29 watts and each 60-watt light bulb at 39 watts, for total of 146 watts. The other two bulbs shown run normally, being from the good black hot. The result of this kind of condition is that a water heater automatically turning on, or a person turning an electric oven on, will make dead lights run dimly. Lights will go back off when 240-volt items turn off.

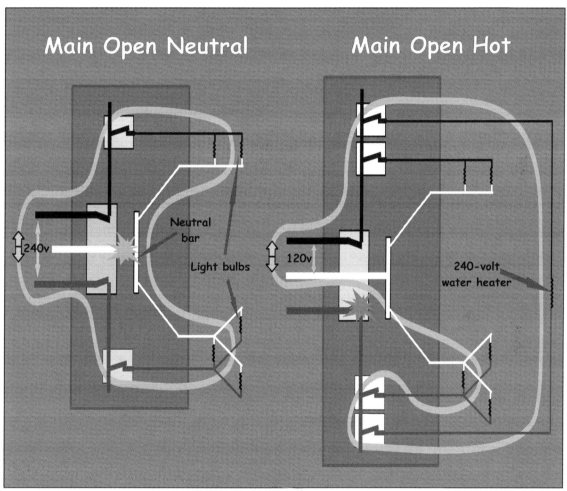

The light-gray loops show roughly the path that current takes when main wires become open. The explosion marks are to show examples of where these opens can occur.

In my experience it is more common for a main open – neutral or hot – to occur along the power company's lines and connections than in the panel or main breaker of a home, which I depicted above. Therefore, if your home's electrical symptoms correspond to either type of main open, I generally recommend calling the power company first. In the case of an open main hot, reasons not to call them would be any indications that the problem is likely inside the home. For instance, if there are main or submain fuses and they have not been checked, or if some 240-volt appliance still operates completely properly. For example, a 240-volt dryer heats up and also turns its drum.

Opens in Submains and Subpanels

Many homes built before 1985 had no single main breaker or main fuse-set. Instead there is a "submain breaker" [134] or "lighting main" or a two-cartridge-fuse pull-out. These do not kill power to all circuits when they are turned off, but only to most 120-volt circuits in the same panel. Where this sort of arrangement exists, an extensive outage or flickering in the house can be due to a tripped submain or a compromised connection at it. Connection trouble at a submain will not usually result in an open-main-hot scenario as described above. This is because there is not usually a 240-volt circuit among those fed by the submain. Nor will an open-main-neutral problem occur for a submain-fed section of circuits, because there is no submain neutral, only the main neutral for the whole panel. However, if a set of breakers is located in a separate subpanel and is fed from a double-pole breaker in the main panel, then the symptoms of either type of main open will be possible for the circuits of the subpanel when the wires or breaker feeding it have trouble.

CHAPTER 9

Pitfalls in Replacing Devices or Upgrading

At some point in a home's life, installing new receptacles, switches, and light fixtures will be a good idea. The originals may be out of fashion, but they also wear out regardless. The homeowner replacing outlets and switches without a glitch is rare. Here are some of the things that can happen.

Switched Outlets

Replacing outlets relies on making new connections. These may be done poorly or wrongly. More than one electrical item may fail to work as a result of a single mistake. An easy goof comes when replacing a receptacle, half of which has been controlled by a wall switch. The upgrader may be aware that the outlet has been switched [110] in this way and may duplicate the exact connections of the old one. But they may not know to break off the metal tab on the hot side of the new receptacle, which isolates the top and bottom halves. The result would be a switch that has no effect: all the formerly switched outlets will always be hot. Kitchens wired in the 1960s may have a similar, easily missed complication [36].

Outlet Hookups

Other problems in replacing outlets come from forgetting to reattach a wire or attaching it in the wrong place. The number, color, and function of the wires at an outlet can be confusing if the original connections are lost track of. Whether the attachment method chosen is screws, push-in holes, or pigtailing [93] with wire connectors, enough insulation must be stripped off the wire for good metal-to-metal contact. Wires should be tugged on to check tightness.

Be aware also of two other matters to do with new receptacles. First, only 14-gauge wires – not 12-gauge anymore – may be inserted in the "quick-wire" holes available on the back of many receptacles. Second, there is a different kind of hole on the back of some styles of receptacle that will not hold on even to 14-gauge wires; these rely on your tightening the side-screws to hold the wire solidly.

Switch Connections

Switches present difficulties as well. The most common mistake can happen when the old switch had three, rather than two, black wires connected to it, even though it was a regular single-pole switch [13]. When you connect to the new single-pole switch, you can get confused by the new green screw they come with, and hook one of those blacks to it. The result will be:
- The switch's light and some things in nearby rooms don't work, and the switch-frame is able to shock you!
- Or the switch's light works from the switch, but some things in nearby rooms don't work
- Or the switch's light stays dead but the switch turns some things in nearby rooms on and off.

Don't connect any black to the green screw. That screw is meant to be given a (bare) ground wire attached to the bundle of grounds, if any, in the back of the electrical box. Instead, two particular blacks should connect to the non-green terminals at one end of the switch and the third to the other end, like they were on the old switch. You may have to try up to three combinations before you get all things working right.

3-way Switch Confusion

The three-way switches that control lights from both ends of a room or hallway are easy to hook up incorrectly. This is absolutely the case if the new switches are not the three-way type, which have three screw terminals that are not green. But even a new three-way switch may have a different alignment of screws than the old. Hint: attach the two wires which come from the same cable as each other, to the two screws that are the same color as each other. See [24].

Light Fixture Replacement

Replacing light fixtures is not foolproof. Sometimes the wiring at a light box is passing the circuit through to various outlets in the area. So care must be taken to connect everything back as it was. Also, an old light fixture may be hiding a surprise. Upon taking it down, you may find the ceiling and wires crisp from years of heat generated by bulbs of too high a wattage. An electrician is often needed to make a good repair in such cases.

Replacement Strategy

In everything I have said above, I am assuming power is off while things are replaced. However, because connection mistakes are so possible, have a strategy for checking your work as you proceed. For instance, do one room at a time, replacing outlets and other items. Then restore power, checking that everything works right there, and also in nearby rooms, before going on to the next room. Otherwise, you will have much more work to recheck later, with possibly more than one goof to complicate the picture.

Service Upgrades

On the subject of upgrading electrical things in general, I have some words of advice about the electrical service upgrade, also known as an electrical service change or a panel change. **The only clear cases of a service upgrade being necessary** are where the existing one is damaged beyond repair or where greater circuit space or service capacity cannot be achieved in another way. Most other reasons amount to paranoia or resale value and may be promoted by contractors who have a vested interest in advising the upgrade.

Trouble with a circuit tripping from an overload will never be solved by a new panel as such. Many existing panels can be given additional circuits even when they appear to be full. This is because a full-size breaker can often be replaced with two mini-size breakers in the same space in the panel. Or a subpanel can be added and fed from spaces whose present circuits will be relocated to the subpanel.

CHAPTER 10

Labeling Your Electrical Panel

To thoroughly label every circuit in your home will take up more space than is available on your electrical panel itself. On the other hand, **you don't want to keep the record you will make away from the panel**, in a notebook or in a computer, because the next homeowner, or anyone servicing your system, may be deprived of your hard-found data.

So I recommend creating a chart of some kind that will mount to the panel and is proportioned like the layout of the circuit breakers (or fuses) themselves. If it doesn't leave you room for detailed descriptions, have it refer to other pages you will bind with it. I also recommend using pencil rather than ink. Over the life of the house, it will then be easier for people to make changes, additions, or rearrangements.

There are two common ways of numbering the circuits, but if no system is already apparent (e.g., stamped into the metal of the cover), you are free to make up your own. It will help if you give even potential circuit spaces, and half-spaces, their own numbers – up to 40 in many cases.

Now, the best procedure for an accurate inventory of your circuits is a systematic one. Whatever way you go about this task, I want to forewarn you that your work will be incomplete and you will need to repeat steps unless you first determine two things about your entire house.

List Every Item

First you need – for your own sanity – to list each and every electric item in or around your home. You are not going to find that each circuit corresponds exactly with a nameable room. So you need to think in terms of each receptacle, each light, and each built-in appliance. And don't forget things like wired smoke alarms, a security system, the doorbell, a furnace, electric heaters and water heaters, air conditioners, pumps, lights under the house or in an attic, outdoor and garden lights and receptacles, and things controlled automatically by thermostats, photocells, motion sensors, and timers.

Working or Not?

Second, you will need ways to determine whether each of the things listed is receiving power or not. Using a portable lamp or nightlight makes sense for receptacles. Switching most permanent lights on or leaving their switches on makes sense, if your light bulbs are all functional. But other items may take more doing; think ahead about this.

Choice of Procedures

A common reasonable procedure for determining which things a given circuit consists of, is to turn off a single breaker and then go check for what is dead. This will work if you are sure to check everything in the house for deadness. Another way is to turn everything in the panel off – except a main or submain [133] breaker – and then turn on just the circuit to be described. This method forces you to see signs of life in a thing before including it. As with the other method, you still need to check everything in the house. In both cases, after you have identified everything in the first circuit or two, the number of remaining things to keep checking gets smaller. Decide which one method you will use and stick to it.

Things to Consider

Treat 240-volt circuits as a unit. They will be using double breakers, whether as two singles tied together or as a solid double-pole breaker. **A 240-volt circuit might even be running (improperly) from separate single breakers.** For labeling purposes, do not get confused in thinking that these must correspond to 120-volt circuits somewhere.

You might encounter some uncommon results. If there are items which will not turn off for any breaker, or which turn on for more than one, some kind of miswiring has occurred and needs correcting. Another thing to look for would be if one of the large double breakers controls quite a few lights and receptacles – one-third of the house or more. This may indicate that this breaker:

- Is a "submain" [133] (and needs that label) and simply sends its power to most of the single breakers in the panel, or
- Is feeding a subpanel elsewhere in the house, which has a number of circuits of its own. If so, locate and label its breakers, and label the double breaker at the main panel "Subpanel," telling its location.

In labeling your electrical circuits, try to avoid descriptions like "Aaron's room" or "TV room." These designations can change and will be no help to another owner. Try using terms like "receptacles on north wall of west bedroom."

Happy hunting!

CHAPTER 11

Testers

Things *called* testers are hardly the only way to learn the status of things in your electrical system. When they will be helpful, use them according to the manufacturer's instructions, common sense, and safety [5]. Which testers make general sense for some purposes will be explored here. Later on, you will be more ready to consider how best to test for very particular purposes [63]. The following chart will introduce you to some of the most common, available, and simple testers:

TESTER ↓	GOOD FOR	LIMITATIONS	HOW TO USE
Electrostatic wand =volt stick =noncontact voltage tester	Indicates presence of hot without direct contact	Not reliable close to earth; can't distinguish within bundle of wires; sensitive to a range of volts and phantom [65] voltage	Hold wand near wire or cable at different angles till light or indicator stays on
Neon tester	Hot presence pinpointed; relative brightness for different voltages	Good reading doesn't mean load will run; may read phantom voltage	Touch one prong to hot, the other to yourself or something grounded

Three-prong receptacle tester	Quick, usually reliable for hot presence and (if there is a ground) neutral presence; some can also test GFCIs	Depends on ground or neutral presence to work; descriptions [64] can mislead; good reading doesn't always mean load will run; does not tell positively that hotness is absent	Plug into three-hole receptacle, read about resulting lights from list on it
Voltmeter	Volt presence and level	Good reading doesn't mean load will run; may read phantom [65] voltage	Touch one prong to each thing to tell voltage difference between them
Ohmmeter	Continuity and resistance level	Does not tell what the resistance will be under load (e.g., light bulbs, motors)	With circuit off, touch one prong to each thing for resistance between them
Clamping ammeter	Checks overloads and shorts in progress, whether something is running	–	Clamp around single wire, not whole cable or cord
Electromagnetic circuit finder =current tracer.	Can pinpoint which breaker controls a good circuit.	Occasionally inaccurate; only expensive ones can trace wires in walls and underground	Transmitter plugs into receptacle; receiver indicates breaker at panel
"Wiggins" =solenoid voltage tester	Some voltage levels; checks circuit operation under load and presence of good ground; can roughly test GFCI	Does not tell positively whether hotness is present	Touch one prong to each thing to tell voltage difference between them

Light bulb in socket with two wire leads	Checks 120-volt circuit operation under load, presence of good ground; can roughly test GFCI	Does not tell positively whether hotness is present	Touch one wire to hot, one to neutral or ground
Mechanic's Stethoscope	Hears arcing location	–	Touch to nearby non-metal or grounded part; listen
Continuity tester	Tells general continuity	Cannot distinguish between a short and many normal connected loads	With circuit off, touch one prong to each thing for continuity (or not) between them
Multimeter	Combines voltmeter and ohmmeter	–	See ohmmeter and voltmeter

A tester is like a question. If you don't ask the right question, the answer may be puzzling. The brief comments in the chart above are to guide you, generally, in picking the right tester for the right question. Sometimes more than one tester will need to be used, and sometimes only in a certain order. So my further comments here will elaborate what the chart says and alert you to issues you may not be aware of. I am writing in general about what sort of tests are needed for different situations. For specific suggestions on good ways to test for different things you are welcome to consult "How to Test for What" [63]. But I think it will help if you first understand the logic behind those suggestions.

Anytime you are about to use a tester – I could say "are *tempted* to use a tester" – **ask yourself what your purpose is**. Suppose that you answer that you want to know, "Is this thing hot?" Even within this question there are different possible purposes. You may just want to know if you are personally safe handling a wire, screw, etc. Or you might want to know as part of troubleshooting a problem, whether you are dealing with a healthy hot wire that is capable of doing its job in the circuit. Or instead, you might have a reason to be interested in how hot it is, interested in measuring its degree of hotness – its voltage. But these different purposes call for different testers. There is no generic "hotness tester." This is because the concept of hotness is not clear until a person clarifies their intent.

So, for instance, a non-contact tester or a neon tester can tell you when it is probably safe and when it is probably not safe to touch a wire. Other testing can make these probabilities certain. But these two testers cannot determine for you whether a wire they say is hot can carry more than a tiny bit of current, because they don't use much (neon) or any (non-contact) current themselves. Sometimes a poor connection upstream from a wire that registers as hot this way, won't let enough current through to run anything important.

Other testers that don't draw much current are the 3-prong receptacle tester and the voltmeter. So they can't tell us that a circuit is good in every respect, but they will tell us if a circuit is bad in some respects.

On the other hand, a solenoid-type tester or an ordinary turned-on lamp will tell whether the circuit, at that point, is capable of running a load. But when they don't light up or vibrate, this is not, by itself, any indication that everything there is dead and safe.

Of the six testers mentioned so far, only the first two can indicate some hotness independent of the presence of a good ground or good neutral. The non-contact and neon testers can do this by using your body as a slight source of ground. When the other four testers fail to show voltage between wires, they do not automatically let you know which is bad, the hot or the neutral/ground. The 3-prong tester attempts to overcome this difficulty by simultaneously checking voltage from the hot to each of the other outlet holes – neutral and ground. This does enlighten you if at least one or the other of those holes is indeed grounded. But if neither is grounded, the tester is suggesting that the hot hole isn't hot – "open hot" – which may not be true at all. For the ins and outs about 3-prong testers, see [63].

The last two I want to comment on are the ohmmeter and the continuity tester. They both try to send battery current through a path by connecting to two points believed to be two ends of such a path. Unlike the testers above, then, these two are primarily power sources. They let you know if their power has succeeded in finding a complete path, by using that power to move a needle or light an indicator bulb. I do not find the continuity tester as helpful as an ohmmeter because the continuity tester will light up – or buzz, if it is that type – for paths that have a certain level of resistance but not for resistances that are a bit higher. Even the times I use an ohmmeter are usually limited to checking if an ordinary light bulb or fuse is bad.

If I am checking a switch, I usually have a 120-volt hot available and simply see if it gets through the switch when On and not when Off. If I want to see if a wire at one outlet goes to another outlet, I tend to use a 120-volt source. Continuity and ohm testers might be used for the same purposes with the circuit off, but I see them as notoriously confusing unless the person knows exactly what the results will mean in each situation. **Performing tests just out of curiosity is generally distracting.** To understand the readings you get might mean mapping out an entire circuit and understanding the resistances of many things on that circuit. I think you'd rather concentrate on solving your problem.

TROUBLESHOOTING

CHAPTER 12

A Troubleshooting Strategy

Headings in This Chapter

Troubleshooting in a Nutshell
A Strategy Overview
Narrowing the Cause Category
Pinpointing the Location of the Cause

Troubleshooting in a Nutshell

Here is a quick, concise look at how to find the source of residential electrical problems. For better details, skip to the strategy [51].

If one thing isn't working, turn it on or replace it. If more than one thing is not working, reset breakers and GFCIs. If they still don't work, locate the bad connection by improving connections at the interface between working and non-working things of that circuit, if you know the circuit; or between the non-working things and any nearby working things, if you don't know the circuit. If they still don't work, you can replace the breaker and check the neutral connections at the panel. If more than one circuit is affected, be sure that main and submain breakers are not blocking the voltage; then call the power company.

If the breaker or GFCI retripped upon your resetting, unplug or switch off everything you can on that circuit, if you know it, (otherwise everywhere) and try resetting again. If it holds, see which thing you undid sets it off. But if it didn't hold, break the circuit's hot apart midway along the circuit and try resetting. Continue reconnecting the circuit and breaking the hot apart at other places, one at a time, to narrow down where the fault is occurring. If it was the GFCI retripping, go back after these procedures and break the neutral apart in a similar way in case this will narrow the location down.

If, instead of not working, the problem is that blinking, flickering, dimming, or brightening of lights occurs or that power to some things comes and goes at will, then keep track over time of which lights and even receptacles are affected and which are not. If the irregularity is limited to part of a circuit, improve connections at the interface between the troubled things and the good of that circuit. If it affects the whole circuit, check the circuit's panel neutral or replace the breaker. If the unusual behavior extends to more than one circuit, check all panel neutrals; see if good voltage is sustained at the time of blinks, etc., at all terminals of the main breaker and of any submain [134] breaker. Finally, if these procedures suggest the power company's connections are at fault, have them check their things.

If, instead, someone has been shocked, confirm which thing(s) is hot using a tester, and turn off circuits one by one to see which is to blame. If unplugging, disconnecting or switching off things of that circuit – especially the hot thing – eliminates the hotness, have the item responsible replaced or repaired. Then have the circuit grounded better. But if there was still shock hazard present, break the hot wires apart in various places along the circuit, as outlined above for solving short circuits, but noting instead whether the offender's hotness is affected. If metal piping was hot, check all accessible pipes for contact with cables.

Your troubleshooting can be guided according to your situation, by trying the Diagnostic Tree, Chapter 19 [80], but to guide yourself with greater understanding, continue here.

A Strategy Overview

The Background Section (Chapters 2-11) has given you a picture of the extent and complexity of a home's system. Now you can begin to see how to approach electrical troubleshooting systematically. I do not want to discourage intuition, but it is easy to make false assumptions about what is going on. Therefore, I will lay out here a fairly organized approach that has impressed itself on me over the years, thanks to trial and error. It makes diagnosis more fun, less frustration. The gist of the diagnosis strategy is to put the symptoms in a category, then by tests and logic to determine another category – the category of the cause – and finally, if necessary, to pinpoint the location of the cause by other tests and logic.

1. **The first step I recommend is to observe the problem yourself**, if possible. Do not go blindly by what others have said or by the language they have used to describe the matter. Some troubles only happen once and are gone. Some things thought to be dead are actually working.
2. **Consider what others say about the problem and its history.** Ask them, and yourself, relevant questions. Often the coinciding of the problem with another event is relevant. But often it is not. Take into account what anyone has already done to try to solve things. This will tell you whether layers of complication may have been added to the picture. You may become tempted to think the cause of the problem is clear, and to short-cut a more deliberate approach such as I am giving. If you do go after such a probable cause, take care not to affect the crime scene in a way that will complicate it for you later if you come up empty.
3. **Next try to put the problem's symptoms in a category**. This will help determine what tests can be done to get to the cause. Briefly the basic symptom categories I

suggest are:

a. **Some things don't work**. This is the most common trouble. And when this is the rock-bottom symptom, it is important to recognize it as such. The symptom is not suddenly: "the breaker doesn't work" or "the fixture is bad" or "the switch doesn't work." Those may be possible causes, and therefore replacing such components might take care of the problem. But if you are going to be an effective detective, you need to keep the real mystery – the basic symptom – in mind. Namely: some things are not working. Then you can proceed to test out the various possibilities – and save time and money by not replacing everything in your electrical system.

b. **Things are working now but in the past some things have gone out and later come back on, or else they will blink or flicker at times**. In other words, the failure is intermittent. It is either very brief or longer lasting. If there is blinking, it would be instantaneous – less than a second – and might or might not be related to heavy appliances turning on or off. If there is flickering, it would be irregular or jagged, not rythmic.

c. **Lately, things dim down or brighten up for a time, and sometimes in response to my turning other things on or off**. This category is to be distinguished from the previous one. This is brightness or dimness that may continue for minutes. Then it might fluctuate without warning.

d. **Something won't turn off**. This is a little different from "some things don't work" ("a" above), which refers to lights, outlets, or appliances not running. This category could mean a control device (switch) is not doing its job, but there could be another cause.

e. **Someone experienced a shock**. This is actually quite uncommon compared to the others, but it is the most impressive to a person – impressive about its potential danger and the need to fix the problem.

4. **Now, observe and note the scope of the problem**, regardless of what the symptom-category is. For instance, which lights in the home flicker and which don't? Are there outlets that are dead besides the ones you use and miss the most? This is often very important. Perhaps you should write these facts about the problem down for use in the rest of the diagnostic process. The extent of the problem, along with the category of its symptoms, will help you see what tests to make at what places.

5. **Then use various tests and procedures to narrow down the cause – from a different set of categories – and then to pinpoint its location.** I will describe these procedures below shortly. Here I want to emphasize the frame of mind with which to approach the testing. Carefulness, patience, and confidence are important. Occasionally you will meet with success early in the game, but don't expect this. Again, writing down what you have done and the results you observed may be helpful. Keep noticing your assumptions. Don't introduce more than one variable at a time. To be reliable, electrical diagnosis needs to be somewhat scientific in its method.

6. **Finally, when you have found the nature and location of the cause, take action to correct it.** This may be as simple as resetting or replacing something. Or it may involve cutting damaged wires back a little (with power turned off) and making new connections. I later describe some of these basic repairs [79]. If you reach the point of repair and it seems a little beyond your ability or knowledge, a friend or a professional can be brought in at that point, but you will have done the head-scratching part.

Narrowing the Cause Category

There are several possible causes for a given symptom. The basic symptom does eliminate some causes immediately, as can be seen in this chart:

SYMPTOM →	→		→	→	→
CAUSE ↓	Does not work	Goes off and on at will or flickers	Runs dim or bright sometimes	Won't go off	Shocks
Short/ Ground- fault/ Overload	Yes	–	–	–	–
Circuit or main wire connection open	Yes	Yes partially	Yes	–	–
Ground- fault with no ground	–	–	–	–	Yes
Miswiring	Yes	–	–	Yes	Yes
Mis-set or bad device	Yes	Yes	–	Yes	–

Without knowing the kind of cause at work in your problem, you are less likely to get to the root of it. For definitions of some of these causes, see [130]. How does a person go about identifying which one kind of cause is behind the symptom? To answer this, we need to get specific for each symptom, as follows.

a. **Does Not Work**. Is the cause of this some kind of short, an overload, an open, a miswiring, or a bad device?

   i. A *bad or turned-off device* – other than a bad breaker– will not affect more lights or appliances than the device is supposed to control or serve. But there can be connections at that switch, receptacle or light that could be poor and affect the circuit from that point on.

   ii. A *miswiring* should almost be assumed if the problem's timing corresponds with some home remodeling or some upgrading of devices [41]. By miswiring I mean wrongly connected, not poorly connected. When there is a miswiring, it will be the ultimate cause behind other causes listed in the chart above.

   iii. When some things aren't working, the most important cause to determine or eliminate is the one I lump under the title *short/ground-fault/overload*. I say this because these all result in a tripped breaker (blown fuse) or GFCI. If such trippedness is not discovered early, the cause behind the outage will escape you. In fact, finding and attempting to reset these can quickly lead to knowing which of these three subcauses is operating. Namely, a breaker or GFCI that lets itself be reset indicates that there had been, respectively, an *overload* or a non-recurring *ground-fault*. (One exception about the breaker that allows resetting is if it sometimes gets hot during normal loads because of a poor connection at it; this will make it false-trip at times [85].) On the other hand, if the resetting results quickly in a retripping, then you have a *short* or, if a GFCI is retripping, a light-weight *ground-fault*. Because the trippedness of a device is so crucial to know, I want to insist you go to "Has Something Tripped?" [62], to make certain you can confirm or eliminate the matter of tripping, because these devices are often hard to locate, reset, or interpret.

iv. An *open* is most likely the cause of an outage if the other causes above (i., ii., iii.) have been ruled out. But independently, an open neutral is almost certain if hotness is still present at a non-working item. A receptacle tester would read "open neutral" or "hot and ground reversed." An open is also likely if the dead items are more than one, but not enough to constitute a whole circuit. Dead outlets in the places [71] required to have GFCI protection, should not be thought to have an open till a tripped GFCI is ruled out.

b. **Goes Off and On At Will or Blinks or Flickers.** Is this symptom due to a partial open in the wiring connections, or something wrong with a device or fixture? If the extent of the blink or outage is limited to one item or one switch's set of lights, then the cause is probably a *bad device* or fixture. If the things affected are more widespread, then the cause will be a connection that is compromised – *partially open* – somewhere. Its location would be one of the connection points [16] along the circuit, at its breaker, or at a main wire. A main wire problem would affect things on more than one circuit.

c. **Runs Dim or Bright Sometimes.** This, indeed, has only one cause-category – an *open*. It may be intermittent or not. Is a main wire – of power company, meter area, or within the panel – having trouble, or is it a circuit wire? If these strange voltages affect things in many parts of the home, a main wire connection [38] is probably poor – often the power company's fault (call them). If it is limited to one or two circuits, then it is probably an open neutral shared by two circuits [36].

d. **Won't Go Off**. Is this from a bad device or a miswiring? *Miswiring* from remodeling or from upgrading of devices [41] should occur to someone right away as a likely cause. Whatever won't go off will be noticed quickly and associated with such recent activity. Aside from miswirings, the cause will be that the *device* that is supposed to shut the thing off is either not adjusted right, or else is faulty and will need replacement. Repair is usually impossible or iffy.

e. **Shocks Someone**. Aside from the rare 240-volt shock, this would by nature be a case of a *ground-fault* finding its only path to ground through a person's body. *Miswiring* is a prior cause that might set up this condition. Rewiring or replacement of devices in a home may be fresh in your mind and suggest good places to look.

Pinpointing the Location of the Cause

Of the causes we have just gone over, the location of some will be clear immediately. This is true of the **bad device**, the **overload**, and some **miswirings**. (Other miswirings may need to be pursued in the manner of a short or open below.) The overload, is a usage problem. You will understand an overload if you learn the extent and capacity of the circuit and compare that to the total wattage of the lights and especially appliances that were running on it. 1800 watts and 2400 watts, respectively, can run on a 15-amp and a 20-amp 120-volt circuit.

The other causes will need further investigation to find the exact place on the circuit that is responsible. These are the **short**, the **ground-fault**, the **shock** (=ground-fault with no ground), and the **open**. So I will go into how to locate these below this chart. (It is the same one you just saw.)

SYMPTOM →	→	→	→	→
CAUSE ↓	**Does not work**	**Goes off and on at will or flickers**	**Runs dim or bright sometimes**	**Won't go off**	**Shocks**
Short/ Ground- fault/ Overload	**Yes**	–	–	–	–
Circuit or main wire connection open	**Yes**	**Yes partially**	**Yes**	–	–
Ground- fault with no ground	–	–	–	–	**Yes**
Miswiring	Yes	–	–	Yes	Yes
Mis-set or bad device	Yes	Yes	–	Yes	–

THE SHORT CIRCUIT. Since the short, the ground-fault, and the shock are all faults, that is, cases of unintended continuity, the procedures for pinpointing their fault-points are similar. In general, this involves isolating parts of the circuit from each other and then retesting for the continued presence of the continuity. While this can be accomplished by a divide-and-conquer approach, I will suggest some more efficient ways as well.

A hot-to-ground short (breaker-tripping ground-fault) is more common than a hot-to-neutral short. It can be helpful to know which you have, and there is a way to know [68].

But let's consider how to attack the short in any case. Most breakers can stand up to repeated shorting, so be ready to keep resetting the one in question. Don't *hold* the breaker on, however; just quickly and firmly push it on.

First, on the dead circuit, **unplug everything and turn all on/off switches off**, and turn only one switch in each 3-4-way system the other way. Try to reset (push off, then on). If the breaker stays on, one of the items you disconnected from the circuit has the short in it, so reconnect one at a time, turning power back on each time. That should identify the culprit. If the short is in a string of lights, keep reading.

But if the breaker retripped in spite of all the disconnections you made, then something more permanent is shorting. I would suspect outdoor things before indoor. In any case, pick a point along the circuit – maybe midway along – and disconnect the hots at that point. This is "divide and conquer." If the short remains, it is electrically closer to the panel than that chosen point. If the short is gone, it is further out. By reconnecting what you undid and then opening new hots in the direction of the short and by keeping track of all this, you should reach a place or a particular length of cable at which to look for the actual short.

If you suspect a recent screw or nail is to blame, see [96]. If the short's location is inaccessible, you might know enough to bypass it with new cable. Overall, if the short circuit just won't reveal its source, a good electrician might be able find it.

THE GROUND-FAULT. By ground-fault here, I mean a ground-fault that has tripped a GFCI receptacle or a GFCI circuit breaker. But realize that a GFCI breaker in the panel could be tripping for an overload or for a hot-to-neutral short instead. Review GFCIs [31].

You have the advantage that the number of downstream loads is limited and their locations are knowable or guessable. Namely, the dead receptacles will tend to be found at the places [71] that were required to be GFCI-protected. You have the disadvantage or complication that the fault could be from hot to ground or from neutral to ground. To determine which it is, you can temporarily disconnect the "load" neutral(s) at the GFCI; if it still trips, the fault is hot-to-ground. Otherwise it was neutral-to-ground. Yes, a GFCI will trip for either condition. Either one provides an alternate path for some of the load current. To the GFCI, some current is missing when it compares the amount flowing on black and the amount on white. If there were no fault, these would be equal.

For either form of ground-fault, **note whether any of the dead receptacles have a cord plugged in and unplug them**. Then see if the GFCI will reset. If not, note whether any of the receptacles are broken and whether they, or the interiors of their boxes, are wet and whether any out in the yard receive their power by a buried cable. Replace any broken ones, dry out the wet things and reset the GFCI. If it still trips, undo the hots and neutrals of the buried cable at the box where it seems to leave the house. Reset the GFCI. If it no longer trips, you need to reconnect and then repeat this disconnecting procedure at other boxes in the yard. If you have found nothing making contact from hot or neutral to ground or earth, then you may find the GFCI still tripping for one particular piece of buried cable. So you would pull up, dig up, and repair or replace that piece.

If the GFCI tripped even when the line feeding to the yard was undone, come back indoors. Open any dead boxes. Look for hot or neutral wires making contact with any ground wires.

THE SHOCK. Caution: this is one problem not to obscrve yourself, at least not by using your body directly. I recommend a neon tester, with one probe held to the palm of your hand, to check bare metal for hotness. A non-contact tester may pick up indications of hotness that are not related to the shock.

For this sort of ground-fault, two strategies are possible. One is to leave the ungrounded fault in place and locate it first, grounding things better later. The other is to provide a good ground to the thing that delivered the shock. This will probably create a breaker-tripping short, and then you can deal with it as a short [56]. Though it feels less safe and I have to be more careful about myself, I find it more efficient to use the first strategy. You should attempt what is safe in your judgment, according to your knowledge. I once had to hunt for a shock condition which had energized all the metal-sheathed cables, all the pipes, and all the ductwork throughout a house and its basement.

If you have decided to leave the shocking thing(s) hot, first see which circuit, when turned off, eliminates the hotness. Get well acquainted with all the other things that are part of that circuit. Then turn it back on. See if those other things show that stray hotness, including the grounding hole of receptacles. If the home was built after the 1960s, hotness is more likely to be limited to one thing or to that fraction of the circuit from which a ground wire has become disconnected. If the home was built before the 1960s, it is likely to spread hotness to various metal things if metal-sheathed cable has lost its contact with ground.

If nothing else but the "shocker" shows hotness, disconnect the hot wire of that one item. If hotness disappears from its shocking metal, then it has the faulting wire or part within it. If hotness persists, then on this circuit unplug everything, and turn all on/off switches off, and turn only one switch in each 3- or4-way system the other way. Did one of these actions eliminate the hotness? If so, it is the home of the shock.

Look along this circuit for any broken receptacles, like where a too-long silver cover-screw may have broken the receptacle's plastic apart. Also, take all covers off receptacles and switches of the circuit, and look for a ground wire curled up next to the hot terminals.

If the shock – the hotness – is not always there, is there some automatic appliance or light that is responsible when it turns on – at certain times of the day, for instance.

Beyond all this, **pick a point midway along the circuit and undo its hot wires there**. If the shock-location hotness disappears, then the fault was coming from somewhere electrically beyond (away from panel) this midpoint. If the shock-place is still hot, the fault is electrically back toward the panel from midpoint. You can reconnect the hots and then repeat this divide-and-conquer procedure at other points to narrow the fault location down. To avoid confusion, record your results as you go.

If nothing leads you to the fault itself, you can give a good ground to the shocking thing, so that a short is created and perhaps trips the breaker. Then troubleshoot it as a short [56].

THE OPEN. I estimate that the chance of an open happening in a given household during its lifetime is at least 50%. Since this is perhaps the most common electrical illness homes suffer, take heart! Hundreds of opens are solved around the country every day, and yours has no reason to be specially stubborn. Since an open is an unintended discontinuity, locating it can involve experimentally disturbing connections till the bad one makes good contact again briefly, or else figuring out fruitful places to look for the discontinuity.

First, you need to learn all you can about the extent of the outage and its circuit, so that you will be ready to probe into enough places and won't have to probe into any uselessly. Do not skimp on this step. Be thorough. You will be comparing the lay of the outage to the lay of the whole circuit.

So your first job is to know the outage. How well would you get to know it if I had to pay you $100 for every dead item you found, but you had to pay me $500 for every one you missed? You are very aware of the lights and outlets you no longer have the services of. What about the ones you never use and the ones behind furniture and stored boxes that you don't even remember exist? Are you going to overlook items that are unique or out of the way: the doorbell's transformer, a wired-in smoke alarm, or junction boxes in the attic or crawl space? Yes, you may have to get more intimate with your home than you were in the past. Document what your new intimacy reveals.

Your next job is to know the outage's whole circuit, if possible. For this you will need this same thoroughness and perseverance you exercised for knowing the outage. Yes, it is most likely that several more things of the circuit in question are still working. Don't rush to see what the labels on your panel say. They won't say enough and might even be lying. You can't afford to base your whole investigation on shaky assumptions. I don't care if you labeled it yourself, back when everything was working. You may have to do a little guessing later on, not yet.

And how can you tell which circuit the outage is part of? If it is the hot wire that is open – not getting through from the bad connection onward – you may not be able to learn its circuit. Yes, you could try to believe the panel, or you could turn off other circuits one at a time and see which one "seems less full" than the others. But you have a 50/50 chance that it is the neutral (white) that is open instead. If it is, you can absolutely know which circuit you are dealing with. You can – if you get a tester. A neon tester, non-contact voltage checker, or (for circuits wired since 1970) a receptacle tester, will let you do this. They cost from $2-$20. How will they tell you whether the neutral is open? By lighting up or beeping when inserted in a non-working outlet or one of its slots. You know the neutral is bad from two facts: that the outlet can't run normal things and that it has a good hot, because the tester lit up. But see [65]. If the hot is good, then all you need to do to identify its circuit is turn breakers off one at a time while continuing to look for the light or beep of your tester.

If you were lucky enough to have an open neutral, don't slack off. Keep your luck going by doing as much research on the full extent of the working items as you did on the non-working ones. Notice, I don't call them dead, because in your case they have a live (hot) wire at them, which is quite able to shock you when you have the circuit on. Again record everything on the circuit that works, including those out-of-the-way items.

Good. And you folks with the open hot, don't despair. You will have your day. And you tester-less people, don't count yourselves out. Now, whether your open is of the neutral or the hot or unknown, you are going to try to disturb the bad connection back into working briefly. **I call this The Jiggle Method.** If you know the circuit's working things from its non-working ones, or can only guess that nearby working things may be part of the same circuit as your non-working things, you can now get down to the real work. Have all circuits turned on. Go plug a working, turned on lamp or nightlight (radio?) – something that will work instantly without a lag – into one of the non-working outlets. (If the outage involves no outlets, turn on the non-3-way switch of a non-fluorescent light within the outage area.) Then assign someone else the job of watching that light constantly and reporting to you immediately if it tries to light up – even the slightest flash. I suppose you could drag a light on an extension cord around with, you all by yourself.

Ready? Position yourself among all the non-working items you discovered. Face toward your electrical panel. As you move in your imagination, without regard to walls and floors, toward the panel, the first working items (of the circuit, if you know it) that you would start to pass into the midst of are crime suspects, along with those non-working items nearest to these working ones. You, the detective, are to go take the covers off all outlets and switches – dead or alive – along this dead/live border [61].

Now use The Jiggle Method. Plug something else into these outlets, one after another, and wiggle it side to side somewhat. Next go back to the same outlets, and also to the switches, and stick a strong, thin stick of plastic or wood, not metal (e.g., a chopstick) beside the device, pressing firmly on the wires you see, and then stick it more behind the device, pressing and poking various wires you can't entirely see. You can even pound on the wall or ceiling near the boxes of this electrical border. The purpose of all these activities is to disrupt wires back into good contact. If at any time your helper tells you the light flashed or stayed on, stop where you are! This is where the connection needs to be improved!

This Jiggle Method will often succeed, but certainly not always. This is the point at which you sad people with the open hot get a shot of hope, and the open neutral folks have to sit down and rest awhile. The reason is, if you invested in one of those non-contact voltage checkers, you can now try letting it tell you where the open hot is. You see, a 50/50 chance has come around to you now. There is a 50% chance that the open is at the first non-working box along the circuit. The other 50% is that it is at the last working one. Therefore, if you were to stick that volt-stick past all non-working receptacles or switches to the wires behind them, you have that 50% chance that it will register steady hotness, telling you that you have found the bad spot! Be sure it gets up against each of the wires in the box. You will probably have to loosen the device from the box, somewhat, to do this. If no non-working device shows this hot wire behind it, then it will probably be one of the exposed working devices that hides the problem. You will need to visually and manually check [77] or improve the black-wire connections at these places, with the circuit turned off.

You open neutral people, however, will have to resign yourselves to checking [77] and improving the white-wire connections at both the non-working and the working places on this dead/live border (shown opposite). Those who cannot be sure what things are part of the outage's circuit will have to check [77] and improve connections of both colors in the general area of the outage and of nearby working things, with circuits off.

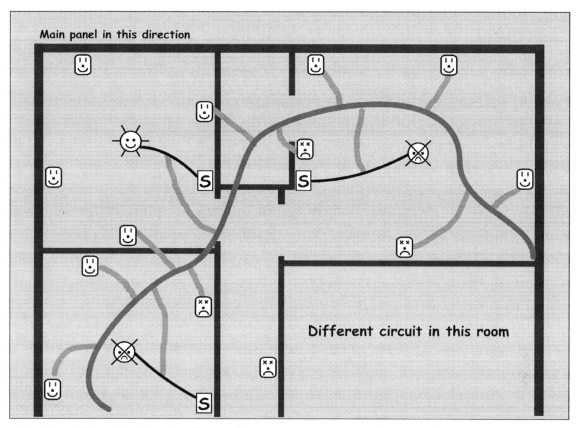

The Dead/Live Border. Dark gray line separates non-working and working items (treat each light and its switch as a unit). Supposing all items shown are the entire circuit, the open connection is probably at one of the items (working or not) as indicated by the light gray lines. A working item can be the location of the poor connection, failing to pass hotness or the neutral on to the wire going to dead items, which is why they are dead. Or else a good hot or neutral arrives at an item but has a poor connection there, which is why it and the things it feeds are dead.

When I say that 50% of the time the open will be found at the first non-working item and 50% at the last working item, I exaggerate only a little. The exceptions are: junction boxes (which can't be said to "work"), rare inaccessible splices or breaks, the chewing of rodents (also rarer than imagined), and underground splices. Nevertheless, generally, the trouble point will be found in electrical boxes, including the panel.

More possibilities. It was common in homes built 1940-1970 to run a circuit through light boxes more than outlet and switch boxes, so there may be connections to be disturbed and checked there. Homes built 1900-1950 may still be relying on their original knob-and-tube wiring connections. If these were not soldered well, they can be the cause of an open. They are not found in electrical boxes but in ceiling and wall spaces. If they are accessible, someone jostling them with a stick could make the light, in The Jiggle Method above, flash on.

A restatement of how to find an open is found at [85]. If you have tried these things without success, a good professional may be needed.

CHAPTER 13

Has Something Tripped?

At your main panel or subpanel or a fuse box, can you easily tell from looking, that nothing is tripped or blown? The answer is "No." If something is obviously tripped or blown, fine (although it could represent an ancient problem someone else gave up on long ago – not your present problem). No, very often something can be tripped or blown and be hard to detect. The surest way to find out is to test for hotness [67] at the circuit wire where it leaves the breaker or fuse terminal; that terminal screw itself is usually just as good a place to test.

If you are avoiding this test from a concern about safety, a second-best procedure is to very firmly push the handle of every breaker, in turn, firmly to full Off, so that it perhaps even clicks in place, and then firmly click it to On. But don't be holding it on, especially if it is buzzing or humming. This is the right procedure for resetting any breaker. "Flip the breaker back and forth" is misleading.

A third-best attempt is simply to weakly press each breaker handle a little more toward On (or later toward Off, but without turning it off) and notice if one breaker seemed to have more give or play to it than the others; then do the off-then-on procedure just on it, remembering which one it is.

Rather than a fuse or breaker, a ground-fault circuit interrupter (GFCI) receptacle could have tripped. Hints for looking for these devices relate to the rooms they are commonly in [71]. Also, at a dead outlet there is a test [71] you can make to tell you how likely it is that it is dead from a GFCI that is tripped somewhere else.

The location of possible tripped devices is not limited to your main panel. Besides reset buttons on garbage disposals, water heaters, and on some in-wall heaters, there can be circuit breakers or fuses in a subpanel far from the main panel. Look in basements, closets, utility rooms and behind pictures, mirrors, and doors. If you have a box of generator switches, one of those might have been knocked off accidentally.

CHAPTER 14

How to Test For What

Headings in This chapter:

Interpreting Outlet Testers
Testing in General
Is a Device or Fixture Good?
Is There Hotness at a Device, Fixture, Box, or Wire?
Is There Neutral or Ground at a Device, Fixture, Box, or Wire?
Testing For Shorts and Ground-Faults

Interpreting 3-Prong Outlet Testers (= 3-Hole-Receptacle Testers)

The arrangement of the three lights on these receptacle testers is different among different manufacturers, but they all have one light to show a voltage difference between hot and neutral slots, another to show a voltage difference between the hot slot and the ground hole, and a third to show a voltage difference between the neutral slot and the ground hole. You could learn the same information by making three tests with the two probes of a neon tester or of a voltage tester.

The three lights of an outlet tester will light up for a range of voltages in the neighborhood of 120 volts, but sometimes a receptacle that is unable to run a lamp can run the outlet tester. That is, under a real load the voltage does not remain as high as it tests. So an outlet that doesn't work might even read "correct wiring."

READING ↓	QUALIFICATIONS
Correct wiring	This is usually accurate. Occasionally the outlet still might not run normal items
Open hot (=no hot available)	This reading can be false if neutral and ground are both poor – a rare condition
Open ground (=no ground available)	Such an actual condition will only give this reading if the neutral and hot are fairly good
Open neutral (=no neutral available)	Such an actual condition will only give this reading if the ground and hot are fairly good
Reverse polarity = Hot and neutral reversed (=hot at left slot and neutral at right slot when viewed with ground-hole down)	Such an actual condition will only give this reading if all three wires are fairly good
Hot and ground reversed	Usually just a case of open neutral in which non-working but turned-on items in the outage allow hotness through them onto the white wires of the outage area. Polarity might be reversed too.
Hot on neutral with hot open	Usually just a case of open neutral with reverse polarity

Chart of outlet tester readings

So the 3-prong outlet tester can't always be taken at face value. There are other rare conditions that can give the same readings as these seven, and further testing, as outlined in the rest of this chapter, can discover these. Having said this, these outlet testers are handy and usually are telling the truth – if you know how to interpret what they are saying. Learn more and see diagrams about the usual causes and implications of the readings at [73].

Your outlet tester may do double-duty as a **GFCI outlet tester**, simulating a ground-fault by the push of a button on it. There is a limitation here. Unlike a good GFCI, which can test itself even without a good ground, the three-prong GFCI outlet tester depends on a good ground to purposely trip the GFCI. This is also true when it is used to try tripping the GFCI by pushing the tester's button at standard receptacles wired downstream from the GFCI.

Testing in General

Review the various testers and the logic behind using each at [46]. Shortly, I will suggest how to test various electrical devices and conditions. First, here are two things to note and some general testing principles.

One note is on testing for "hotness" and "neutralness." Most often when testers indicate the hotness or neutralness of a wire, this will also mean that the wire will be able to carry the current needed to run lights and appliances. **But occasionally the wire will not sustain the needed voltage; contact is poor somewhere.** Even 120 volts measured by a voltmeter may shrink down instantly when a real-life load tries to run. (The rest of this chapter will not generally take this condition or the next one into consideration.)

In addition, many testers may encounter a different condition, **"phantom voltage"** [133][67]. It will tend to register as 50 volts or less but might read almost as high as the usual voltage of the home (120 volts). It would not be able to shock you. It seems to be generated onto a wire that is neither hot nor neutral, by a hot wire that is bundled with it – in the same cable, for instance. To be sure a reading is phantom, see that it will not run a light bulb, then that it does not spark when shorted to ground. Then ignore it.

This chart summarizes some testing issues. It may help clarify your testing purpose.

PURPOSE OF TEST ↓	Points of contact	Tester	Notes
A. **1. Shock hazard** **2. Identity** **3. For hotness, which might be able to carry load**	1	Neon Non-contact	Testers are looking for hotness. Identity includes which circuit (if hotness found) and (if not) extent of problem. This use of neon tester puts one probe in palm of hand (no danger with home voltage).
B. **For voltage difference between points (both points might be able to carry load)**	2	Neon Volt 3-prong	These tests are relative and may need confirmation by A or C. 3-prong outlet tester reports three 2-point relations. Volt tester can be a multimeter.
C. **For ability to carry load (to work)**	2	Items of circuit Bulb Wiggins	These show functionality, not polarity or safety. If hot is identified by A, good ground or neutral is confirmed if this test works.

For outages, you might use the chart above generally as follows. After confirming with C that there is a problem, start with A and work your way from there to B to C again. If B indicates that something should now carry a load (work) but C shows that it will not, you can bring a known working non-GFCI hot and neutral via extension cord and perform the C test from it to the supposedly good neutral and hot (respectively), to see which is actually poor. Before doing so, be sure you will not be testing from hot to hot, since 240 volts might be involved and blow out your 120-volt test item (bulb).

Is a Device or Fixture Good?

Is a receptacle working? Best is to plug a good lamp or appliance in and see. A neon, receptacle, or volt tester may be handier but they don't pull enough current to be sure the voltage is sustainable.

Is a light working? Screw in a bulb you know recently worked. A fluorescent fixture with more than one tube needs all brand-new tubes to test it reliably.

Is a switch working? If the switch is unable to turn on a good bulb, turn off the breaker, remove the wires from switch, connect those wires to each other, and turn the breaker on. If the item now works, the switch or its connection to the wires was probably bad.

Is a bulb good? Try it in a socket known to work. Otherwise test the removed incandescent bulb with ohmmeter. 4-200 ohms is a good bulb, but some good halogens indicate no continuity. Continuity testers vary and may not answer this question for bulbs of all wattages.

Is a fuse good? Best is to remove the fuse and test it with a continuity tester or ohmmeter; any substantial continuity means the fuse is good. If a round fuse is to be tested while in its fuseholder, slip one probe of a neon tester along side the fuse with the other to the palm of your hand. If it lights up, the fuse is good *if* this is a 120-volt circuit *and if* this fuse is for the hot, not the neutral; neutrals in some old homes were fused. For a cartridge-shape fuse that is accessible while in place, touch the probes of a neon tester to the ends of the fuse. If no light shows, the fuse is good, otherwise not – assuming at least one end of fuse *is* hot – so check that first.

Is a breaker good? If this question arises from losing power to the circuit, a short, overload, or open is more likely. If more things in the house work with the breaker on than off, the breaker is fine; you have an open. Be sure the breaker isn't simply tripped. Force it firmly into a full Off position, then firmly On. You could repeat this with the wire removed from the breaker, especially if the breaker didn't stay on or you heard a hum or buzz when you put it on. (These make it likely the breaker is fine and is responding to a short.) If you have the wire removed, you may as well do this test also: if the turned-on breaker's screw reads hot for a neon or volt tester, it is probably good. Also try to run a light bulb or Wiggins tester between that screw and a ground in the panel. The breaker is bad if these won't run. But the best all-around test is to move the breaker's wire temporarily to a new or different breaker, turning both off while moving it. With that breaker on, if the problem has gone away, figure the old breaker was bad; otherwise it is good. One more test would be to turn the breaker off, remove it, reset it to On, and check with an accurate ohmmeter between its screw and its bus-clip. It is likely bad if it reads more than 5 ohms.

Is There Hotness at a Device, Fixture, Box, or Wire?

Does hotness reach a certain receptacle or light? If your purpose is personal safety for working on your problem, a non-contact volt stick will alert you if there is some hotness present. (One exception is when you are checking an underground wire or cable you have uncovered.) When your purpose is to check the extent of a circuit or of an open hot, a neon tester will light up slightly for something hot. Have one of its probes in the palm of your hand. A non-contact voltage tester inserted in these same receptacle slots or light sockets will also indicate hotness. This does not tell you whether the outlet or light has a good neutral or ground.

Does hotness reach a certain electrical box or terminal? Having removed the cover, you can touch an in-hand neon or non-contact tester to the side-screw terminals of any switches or receptacles, but to check deeper in a box, the non-contact tester will be the easiest, once you loosen any devices in the way. At a circuit breaker, one neon prong to the breaker's screw and the other in your palm will light it up if hotness is there. Don't trust a non-contact volt tester to help at a breaker since many nearby things are also hot. These tests do not tell you whether good neutrals or grounds are present.

Which wire is hot? A neon tester with one probe in the palm of your hand is best. If it lights up a bit when you touch it to the metal of a wire, at least that wire is hot, whether is it meant to be or not. A non-contact tester isn't always able to be near one wire without also being near others. Also it too often reads a wire as hot which is merely not grounded and has gathered some "phantom" voltage from a hot wire it runs through the house with. An example would be an unhot traveler in a 3-way switch system. When a neutral is open somewhere on a circuit, white wires in the non-working area of the circuit can often read as hot – and are somewhat – in addition to the true hot. And of course, switched wires are hot when switched on and not when switched off. The fact that a wire is not hot does not mean it is always that way, nor that it is a neutral.

Is the voltage from hot to neutral too high or low? A voltmeter would be touched between hot and neutral. 120 volts, or 240 for special items, are nominal normal voltages supplied by the power company. The actual measured voltage at your home will be a little different – as much as about 5% higher or lower. More variation than this is abnormal. It could be something the power company should correct, or it might indicate a neutral connection problem in one of your circuits [36] or in your main wires [38].

Is There Neutral or Ground at a Device, Fixture, Box, or Wire?

Does "neutralness" reach a certain receptacle or light? If you trust the hot there, plugging in a lamp or screwing in a good bulb shows whether the neutral is good. If the hot is questionable, bring a good hot via an extension cord to where you can attach both it and the neutral in question to the wires of a socket to run a bulb. But see the top of [66]. A less reliable indication that a neutral is healthy is if a continuity tester or ohmmeter shows continuity between it and the ground wire. This should be done with the breaker off.

Does neutral reach a certain electrical box? Approach this as stated for the previous question. However, the neutrals at switch boxes are often less accessible for contacting or attaching to. In such cases, wire connectors may have to be undone to test. The breaker of the circuit(s!) involved in the box should be off until everything is ready for the testing. If neutrals are separated in order to test, it is normal, if you think about it, for only one of these whites to then test out as a good neutral.

Is a ground wire good? If a light socket and bulb attached from hot to neutral works, and also works attached from hot to ground, the ground is good. If it works from hot to neutral, but not from hot to ground, the ground is bad. An outlet, neon, or volt tester may indicate some groundedness, but these do not tell you for sure that a ground is solid. For what to do about a bad or missing ground, see [74].

Testing For Shorts And Ground-Faults

Is a hot-to-neutral short present? The breaker itself – tripping off – is the best test of the shorting. If the circuit uses a fuse, don't repeatedly replace it to test the short unless you use a main pull-out or disconnect ahead of it to recontact the short. The arcing of a short would do damage to a round fuse's holder. The matter of whether it is the neutral that the hot is shorting to can best be determined by disconnecting that circuit's neutral from the panel's neutral bar, capping it, and seeing that the short is then gone. An ammeter clamped on the hot wire at the breaker or fuse can also confirm that it is tripping/blowing for high current. Clamped on the circuit's neutral, it would also show that the short is indeed running hot-to-neutral. An ohmmeter showing 0-5 ohms between suspected wires will tend to mean the short is still there, but since lightbulbs and motors out on the circuit could give such a low resistance reading, I recommend against giving such a test much weight. Give a continuity tester even less weight for the same reason.

Is a hot-to-ground short present? If a breaker or fuse has been tripping/blowing, it will be the best indicator, and a procedure corresponding to that mentioned above regarding the hot-to-neutral short, will apply. But if the fault only trips a GFCI receptacle, that is the best indicator

Is a neutral-to-ground fault present? No regular breaker will trip for this. A GFCI receptacle or breaker will, and is the best way to keep testing. If an ohmmeter showed up to 30,000 ohms from ground to load white(s) (disconnected from the line white), this *might* mean the fault is present.

Is this receptacle dead from a tripped GFCI somewhere? A GFCI receptacle disconnects both hots and neutrals when it trips. So an ohm or continuity check between the neutral slot and the ground hole of a totally dead regular-looking receptacle will tell whether a tripped GFCI is likely. Normally a dead receptacle with no hotness still retains continuity between neutral and ground (assuming the ground is good), since both are connected at the neutral bar in the panel. But one that is downstream from a tripped GFCI will show no real continuity. See [71].

CHAPTER 15

Locating and Troubleshooting GFCI Receptacles; GFCI Code History

If you are pretty sure you need to troubleshoot a ground-fault condition itself, see [57]. Otherwise, keep reading. First, this chart is a summary for troubleshooting the health of a GFCI receptacle [31] device:

CAUSE ↓	GFCI SYMPTOM → → →				
	Pushing test does not pop reset out	Reset won't stay in when pushed	Reset is out but things plugged in work	Reset is in but things plugged in don't work	Reset pops out when something is turned on
Ground-fault down-stream	–	Yes	–	–	Yes
Line and load reversed	–	since 2003	Yes	–	–
Other miswiring of GFCI	–	Yes	–	Yes	Yes
120 volts not reaching GFCI	Yes	since 2003	–	Yes	–
Button not pushed in well enough	Yes	Yes	–	–	–
Defective GFCI	Yes	rare	rare	Yes	–

GFCI receptacles rarely fail. Many other conditions can make it seem as if they are not doing their job when they really are.

When homes are upgraded, people often think GFCIs need to be added in bathrooms and elsewhere. They are under the impression that the outlets there are not already protected. This may not be true. It doesn't actually hurt to double-protect, but it can get confusing. For instance, if something at the bathroom outlet tripped a GFCI, it could trip the device that had been added right there as an "upgrade," or else it would trip the original one in the garage – whichever one happened to respond more quickly. If you don't know the complication, you won't be looking in the right place to restore power.

If your GFCI is giving trouble, can you tell the difference between its tripping and its simply failing to reset? The reset buttons of newer GFCIs (from 2003 on) will purposely not catch hold if they are not receiving power or are not hooked up right. A tripping button, on the other hand, will generally catch hold for a split-second or at least make a mechanical sound when you try to reset.

I have found that some of the Leviton GFCIs can be tricky to reset fully. If you push that button in more on one side than the other, it may not reset both the hot and neutral contacts. Just retrip it with the test button and try again.

Is a GFCI to Blame for an Outage?

When a GFCI outlet trips off, both the hot and neutral "line" terminals become disconnected inside the receptacle from the "load" terminals. Because this is true, there is a test that can determine the likelihood that a tripped GFCI has caused an outage affecting standard receptacles elsewhere:

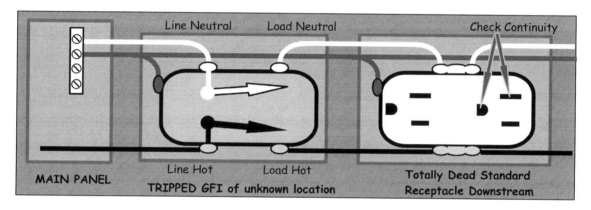

Normally there is continuity between the neutral and ground at a receptacle, because both are ultimately attached to the neutral bar at the main panel. However, if a GFCI receptacle has interrupted power to other normal receptacles, one result would be that a continuity test between neutral and ground at the normal receptacle would show very high resistance (no continuity). With such a discontinuity, one could not be certain it was due to a tripped GFCI, since a poor ground or other condition could show the same result. Nevertheless, it would make a tripped GFCI very likely as the cause, especially if the normal receptacle is located where Code required GFCI protection.

GFCI Code History

Hunting for a GFCI of unknown location takes some persistence, but it can often help to know the history of GFCI requirements in the National Electrical Code (NEC). For U.S. homes, the Code began requiring GFCI protection for receptacles outdoors in 1973 and in bathrooms in 1975; at that time this was more often achieved by a GFCI breaker in the panel rather than a GFCI receptacle. In 1978 garage receptacles were added to the list, and the use of receptacle-type GFCIs became more common. The 1987 Code called for kitchen-counter receptacles within six feet of the sink to be protected. 1996 saw all the kitchen counter receptacles come under the requirement. Outlets in crawl spaces, unfinished basements, and near wetbars were added in 1990 and 1993, and those within six feet of laundry or utility sinks in 2005. See next page.

GFCI Locations in a Home

Because GFCI receptacles are an extra expense and take more labor to install, one GFCI device was typically placed where it could feed protection on to the other normal-looking outlets required to have protection. **Until 1987, this could be achieved by just one GFCI for the whole house.** Then there needed to be more, because kitchen outlets were already required to be on at least two circuits dedicated to the kitchen/dining area. When all the kitchen outlets needed protection (1996), there always had to be at least two GFCI devices for the kitchen, besides at least one for garage/outdoor and one for bathrooms. None of the above may be accurate for Canadian homes; I do not know the Canadian code history enough to give a similar description.

When searching for a hidden GFCI, consider the following. Any circuit, or any part of one, was *allowed* to be protected. In practice, only the ones required to have protection tended to be wired downstream from a GFCI device. But it was sometimes convenient to plant the GFCI device at a location not requiring protection. For example, in the dining room for protecting the kitchen, or indoors for protecting an outdoor outlet. Another common practice has been to avoid giving protection to a refrigerator, since protecting it is not required.

Two commonly overlooked GFCI locations are a rarely-used main-floor guest "powder room" and the garage. The garage is especially worth combing if the electrical panel is there. A circuit for many of the locations requiring protection would naturally begin by going from the panel to a garage outlet, where the device itself would be placed. Garage outlets become invisible in two ways. Literally, they disappear behind stored things or permanent shelves. Psychologically, some of them become forgotten because they have never been actively used. Garage outlets were often placed about four feet above the concrete floor.

CHAPTER 16

Outlet Corrections
From Home Inspections

A home electrical inspection for real estate purposes will often reveal defects the homeowner was unaware of. Many of these are Code violations. Some raise real safety concerns. Others do not. Here I am addressing only the common corrections or recommendations that home inspectors call for in regard to the proper connection, GFCI-protection, or functionality of receptacles in homes. Because some of these corrections will involve a knowledge of circuits and a troubleshooting strategy, this guide as a whole will be of value for making corrections.

Many of these inspector recommendations are generated by their 3-prong outlet testers, which also often test GFCIs as well. I discuss the meaning and limitations of what these testers say at [64]. Here I describe their usual meanings and their correction.

"Open Hot"

 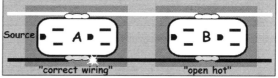

This means the receptacle is dead from the "hot" wire (usually black) not actually being hot. In the illustration above, the left-hand scenario shows the bad connection being at outlet B, which is the outlet that reads "open hot." The right-hand one shows the bad connection being at outlet A, which actually reads "correct wiring" itself. See [58] for how to find an open and [81] to be sure a breaker or GFCI is not the cause.

"Open Neutral"

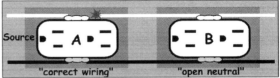

This means the receptacle is not working because, even though the black wire is hot, the white wire is not connected well somewhere, so that it cannot carry any current between there and the main panel. In the illustration above, the left-hand scenario shows the bad connection being at outlet B, which is the outlet that reads "open neutral." The right-hand one shows the bad connection being at outlet A, which actually reads "correct wiring" itself. To find an open, see [58].

"Open Ground"

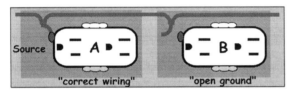

This means good grounding is not reaching the receptacle's round hole, whether or not any wire is connected to its green screw. As with the open hot or neutral, an open ground can be happening at the receptacle itself (or its box) – B of the left-hand scenario above. Or it can be at an outlet "upstream" – A of the right-hand one. With grounds, an open is often a case of someone simply never connecting a ground to the receptacle or forgetting to reconnect if they had occasion to disrupt it. If several outlets near one another show "open ground," there might be a single place where a connection of ground wires (or metal-sheathed cables) has come apart, and this place could be at one of these, or it could be at another nearby outlet that reads "correct wiring."

Another common reason for an open ground is that the home was built before ground wires were required in circuits – before the mid-1960s – and **someone has since installed a grounding-type receptacle without providing a real ground.** In that case, it should be replaced with a two-hole receptacle, or given a ground wire that is connected ultimately to the panel, or given GFCI protection upstream from it. In this last option, Code allows these 3-hole receptacles to remain even though there really is no ground available at them.

"Hot and Ground Reversed"

Usually this is just another case of Open Neutral. The different reading is from the fact that somewhere among the non-working parts of the circuit an electrical item is trying to run and so is letting the hotness from the hot wire through itself onto the white wire. Since the white wire is "open" – not connected well – somewhere between there and the main panel, it shows this hotness at the normally "neutral" slot of the receptacle and gives this odd reading. So treat this as an open neutral.

"Reverse Polarity" = "Hot and Neutral Reversed"

This condition lets the outlet run things, but there can be circumstances in which this would not be entirely safe. It means that the right-hand (shorter) slot of the receptacle – viewing the three holes as a face – is connected to wires that are actually neutral, whereas that slot is supposed to be for hot wires. And the left-hand slot is connected to hot wires instead of neutrals:

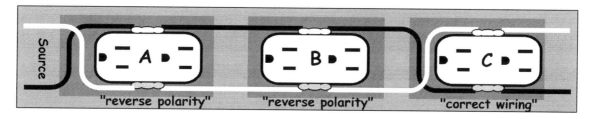

In this diagram, whoever connected outlet A put the black on the white's side and vice versa. They also hooked B up this same wrong way, but for some reason hooked up C right. So C reads "correct wiring" and A and B read "reverse polarity." The solution here is simply to move all blacks and whites at reverse-polarity outlets to their correct side.

But let's consider a complication. There is another, less common way that reverse polarity tends to come about. It is where someone installing or replacing a receptacle, or even trying to correct polarity, connects the white of a black-white pair to a terminal where another black was (see A below) and the black of the pair to the terminal where a white already was.

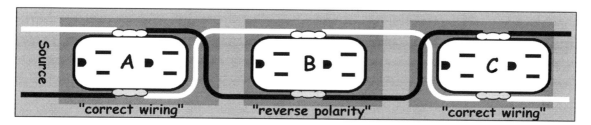

The effect of this, as shown here, would be a polarity reversal in the color-coding of the wires themselves. The polarity would then read "reversed" or "correct" at the receptacle these wires attached to next, depending on whether they attach there according to color (B) or according to actual hotness (C), respectively. Both A and C are reading "correct wiring" in spite of the fact that some wires at them are the wrong color. I will not try to advise you on straightening this sort of thing out, except to say that you may want to start from scratch. Make sure every receptacle along the circuit has whites on the white side and blacks on the black side and that the blacks, and only the blacks, end up actually hot.

"Hot on Neutral with Hot Open"

This configuration of lights is not referred to on all outlet testers. It is usually just a case of open neutral plus reverse polarity, and would be rare.

GFCI Protection Recommended

A home electrical inspection will often result in a recommendation to give certain outlets GFCI protection. You can learn more about when and where Code required GFCI protection in homes at [71]. Here I bring up the point that inspectors should distinguish between the places your home should have had this protection from the beginning, and where they merely recommend having it. In most jurisdictions there is no requirement for a home, even when changing owners, to meet current Code in this matter, as long as no original receptacles were replaced at a time when GFCI protection had become required for them. Of course, you may not want to spend time fighting a buyer over the importance of the inspector's recommendation.

Also understand that GFCI receptacles do not necessarily need to be installed at every location you decide to protect. Often a GFCI receptacle installed at one point (say, in a kitchen) will be able to protect several other normal receptacles in the area, if you connect it in a particular way. See diagram at [31]. Be warned also that there are several wrong ways to hook up GFCIs that will result in their tripping or not working [70].

CHAPTER 17

How to Recognize the Bad Connection in a Circuit

What Are We Looking For?

This chapter is not about whether you have a bad connection [80] or about finding which electrical box to look for it in, [58]. It is about what you are looking for *in* a box – how to recognize which connection there is poor – so that you can make the right improvement or repair.

What Can Be Bad?

At an electrical box, a wire can be loose in, or pulled loose from, its device-terminal or its wirenut. The metal quality of its connection can have deteriorated from heat/corrosion, so it is no longer able to conduct current. Or, not often, a wire can be broken at the terminal or wirenut – usually from being nicked, back when, by the wireman's stripping tool.

Many resources, both online and in books, give the impression that you will find soot, burn marks, or melted wires at the site of an open in the electrical circuit. Actually, it is much more common to see very little obvious difference between a good connection and a bad one. This does not mean we can't find out what is bad, however.

Of course, if you know you are at the right electrical box from testing and your brilliant deductions, then you could just make all new connections in that box. You don't have to ponder what the exact trouble was. But by the time you have come this close to the culprit, you may want to try to understand what happened.

Obvious Signs of a Bad Connection

Yes, there might be ugly evidence of the trouble. See this photo [119]. Often enough, an open will have created some heat. Before things stopped operating, this connection was still carrying current, but through imperfect contact at this point. Current flowing through unintended resistance typically gives you arcing and/or heat. This isn't something that happens overnight. Overheating connections often take years to reach the point of disrupting the path of current entirely. Look for things like these:

- A receptacle, switch, or wirenut that has charred, melted, or fallen apart.
- Wire insulation within 1"-2" of a connection point, that looks melted or cracking.
- White or red wire insulation that is brownish near its connection.
- Discoloring or bubbling on the face of a receptacle or its cover. This only confirms you are at the right box.
- Heat felt on the face of a receptacle or the smell of ozone or plastic vapor there. These signal an active poor connection, one that is still running current through it, one that might become an open in the future.
- Corrosion or rust right at the device's terminals or within a wirenut. Such corrosion elsewhere in the box might not be related to your problem, however.

Don't pay much attention to:

- Burn marks, weld marks, melted metal, or soot. These are typical of the sudden intense heat of a short circuit (from the past), not your present connection problem.

Subtle Signs of a Bad Connection

An open on a electrical circuit often gives little or no visual evidence of its presence. Why some do and some don't is a question for engineers and forensic experts. If you look closely, are there particular things to expect to find? Don't look for just anything odd. Look for:

- Wires ready to pull out of their holes (so tug on each one).
- A broken wire. It might even be broken inside its insulation. Flex or tug at it.
- Dulled and darkened metal of a screw- or hole-terminal (compare with the others on the device).
- A small dark arc-mark near the metal end of a push-in-the-hole wire, once you have removed it.
- The slight smell of burnt plastic when your nose is up to the box. This only confirms you are at the right box.

No Sign of a Bad Connection

This is often the case with push-in-the-hole connections of a receptacle. It is also common enough when one wire in a wirenut didn't stay lined up (slipped a little back) when the wirenut was being twisted on the group of wires. These kinds of connections in the box may all need to be checked, undone, and done over. Then you'll know if you were right about which box had the problem in it!

If you did see evidence of where the problem was, you will likewise be replacing at least anything that was affected – receptacle, wirenut, etc. – anything that suffered visibly from heat or is felt to be unreliable based on this performance.

CHAPTER 18

Repairing

There is usually no reason to repair or replace anything with the circuit still live, and a good reason not to – your safety. Also, some timers, dimmers, photocells, and motion sensors have fragile components that can be damaged if connected to a load while live.

Repair will involve separating a wire from something, improving a wire's connection, and/or replacing a device or connector. If damage has visibly occurred to a wire, it can usually be cut back or sometimes taped up, to restore insulation. If a device has suffered from heat, corrosion, or arcing, replacement is usually called for.

To remove wires from pushed-in-the-hole terminals of receptacles and switches, depress the release near the hole using a very small screwdriver, and pull on the wire. If this does not work, try rotating the device back and forth while pulling back on the wires. Beyond this, just cut the wires loose, close to the device.

Some Specific Tips

If a breaker's connection to its bus bar in the panel has been arcing, simply putting a new breaker there will not be a lasting fix. The bus bar will have been damaged at that point too and will recreate an arcing condition before long with the new breaker. Relocate the new one, if possible.

When reconnecting wires to a new receptacle, I recommend not using the push-in wire terminals on the back of the receptacle. Instead, either use the side-screws (copper curled clockwise under them, with no insulation trapped under the screws) or else pigtail [93] one hot and one neutral from wirenuts to the screws.

When replacing switched receptacles [110] and double-circuit receptacles [36], you need to remember to break off the tab on the hot side, so top and bottom halves don't interact. Do not break off the neutral-side tab.

Splices underground need special connectors. Splices involving aluminum wire do too. Aluminum wire connected directly to receptacles or switches call for these devices to be specially rated for this.

SPECIFIC HELP AND MISCELLANEOUS

CHAPTER 19

A Home Electrical Diagnostic Tree

This diagnostic tree for home electrical problems is largely self-contained. It refers you mostly to other parts of itself. It assumes little special knowledge or tools. It cannot address every problem. If none of the starting choices below apply, or if going through the diagnostic tree does not uncover the source of your problem, try other parts of this guide as a whole.

TO START, select which ONE of the following best describes your problem:
1. More than one thing does not work, and this doesn't seem to be from a tripped circuit breaker. **Go to 19.1.**
2. Things are working now but in the past have gone out and later come back on, on their own. **Go to 19.2.**
3. A circuit breaker has tripped and won't reset. **Go to 19.3.**
4. A reset button (on a ground-fault outlet) has popped out and won't reset. **Go to 19.4.**
5. Lights blink or flicker at times. (But compare #6 in this list.) **Go to 19.5.**
6. Lights strangely dim down for awhile or stay brightened – for no reason or in response to something else turning on or off. **Go to 19.9.**
7. Only one thing doesn't work (or one set of lights controlled by the same switch). **Go to 19.10.**
8. An electric heater is not working or not controllable. **Go to 19.11.**
9. Someone experienced a shock. **Go to 19.12.**

19.1   More Than One Item Out

Several electrical items in your home are not working. You have the most common troubleshooting problem and the one with the most possibilities. Let's try to narrow things down quickly. See if any of the following sounds like your situation.

You don't think a circuit breaker tripped. However, a recent heavy load (vacuum, hair dryer, rug shampooer, microwave, or carpenter's saw) or a recent burning-out light bulb could have tripped a breaker. Or you may have forgotten a separate subpanel with breakers in the other end of the house behind a picture. Or you may not realize that many brands of breakers do not look to be in a tripped position, when they have in fact tripped [62]. And you can't rely on the labeling in the panel to point you to the breaker that really has to do with your outage.

Consider also that an outage in homes built or remodeled since the mid-1970s can be due to the tripping of another safety device than a breaker: the ground-fault circuit interrupter ("GFCI" = "GFI") [31]. Is your outage limited mostly to outlets, and mostly in bathrooms, garage, or outdoors, or in the kitchen/dining/nook area? If so, then it is very likely that a GFCI receptacle in one of those locations has tripped [71]. We can suspect this even more if recently the weather has been wet, or you have had young guests who could have played with the GFCI's "test" button, or you have had contractors using tools around the home. Few people know the location of all GFCIs in their newer homes.

If little of this about breakers and GFCIs corresponds to your problem, you should probably proceed to grapple with it as an Open at 19.7. But if you think you should look further into the possibility that something is tripped off, continue reading here.

The surest way to see if one of the breakers has tripped (or has another problem) is to take the panel's cover off and test for hotness [67] at every breaker screw. (If one is not hot, reset it in the way I will mention next.) If you avoid doing this first test from a concern about safety or from having no tester, a second best procedure is to very firmly push the handle of every breaker, in turn, firmly to full Off, so that it perhaps even clicks in place. Then firmly click it to On – but don't be holding it on much, in case it wants to retrip for a short. A third best attempt is simply to weakly press each breaker handle a little more toward on (or later toward off, but without turning it off) and notice if one breaker seemed to have more give or play to it than all the others. Then do the firm off-then-on procedure just on it, remembering which one it is.

If any of this restored power, learn why the breaker had tripped at 19.6. If none of this restored power to your dead things, but when resetting you heard a definite hum or buzz or saw a flash of light there, you most likely have a short circuit and the breaker has retripped. Even without these symptoms, a breaker that won't give hotness to its screw, with the wire in it, but will show hotness there if you remove that wire and then turn it on, is tripping for a short. So go to Short at 19.8. If the wireless breaker shows no hotness when reset, it needs to be replaced and possibly in a different location in the panel.

If the breakers are now good and not tripping, but your outage remains, consider if a tripped GFCI is the reason before concluding it is an open. Finding the one GFCI that may be responsible for the outage can take some determination. Is it behind shelves or boxes in the garage? Is it in a rarely used powder room? Is it a rarely used outlet in a bathroom? Is it behind a dining room china hutch or tucked back in an "appliance garage" cabinet in a corner of the kitchen? By 1996 all new accessible receptacles outdoors, at wet bars, in bathrooms, garage, kitchen, dining, nook, pantry, crawl space, and in unfinished basements were to be GFCI-protected. So the GFCI devices themselves tend to be in these places. In regard to the kitchen/dining area, I would look for two, not just one. Also see [72].

If you do find a GFCI whose reset button is popped out, push it firmly in once or twice. If it resets and restores power, you are done. Why it had tripped may remain a mystery. If it pops back out go to 19.4. If it holds in but your outage continues, I suppose you could look for another tripped GFCI somewhere. But it's starting to look like, by a process of elimination, you should go to the Open at 19.7.

19.2   Power in an Area Comes and Goes at Will

You have described an intermittent outage. When a whole set of lights and/or outlets stop working for a time, this is from a poor connection. It is usually at an electrical box or device along the circuit, but possibly at the panel or even on the power company's line to your house. (A single recessed light fixture is designed to go off temporarily when it has overheated; this would be from a wrong light bulb or hot environment.)

It is difficult to find where the bad connection is occurring, except during the times that power is gone. At such a time, go to Open at 19.7. If you have been documenting details about the extent of the outages, you might be able to figure out the best places to look for the bad connection. The tendency is for an intermittent outage to progress before long to a lasting one, after only a few comings and goings. Until then, you can try the procedure in 19.7 for Opens, modified to notice a production of the outage, rather than a production of good power.

19.3   Resetting a Breaker

If you have been resetting the breaker correctly, then either it has a mechanical problem or else it is retripping for a short. Breakers will not necessarily reset simply by being pushed back to On, or even by being "flipped back and forth," whatever that means. The correct, effective procedure is to very firmly push the handle to full Off (don't be shy!), so that it perhaps even clicks in place. Then firmly click it to On – but don't be holding it on much, in case it wants to retrip for a short. If doing this restored your power, learn why the breaker had tripped at 19.6. If it does not restore power, then how will you know if the breaker is truly retripping for a short – that is, doing its job – or is itself unable to hold the On position because it is defective?

One indication of a short going on would be if you heard a definite hum or buzz or saw a flash of light there when trying to reset. Another good way is to take the panel's cover off, remove the wire from that breaker, and see if it resets and stays on now. If you have a tester, also test for hotness [67] at the breaker's screw. If the wireless breaker doesn't reset, or doesn't show hotness, then replace the breaker. If possible, put the new one in a different location in the panel. But if the original does stay on when deprived of its wire, then it has indeed been responding to a short. (You might as well put the wire back into the turned-off breaker again.) In this case, you are ready to go after the Short at 19.8.

19.4   Ground-Faults

When the reset button of a GFCI outlet is pushed in, but continues to actually "pop" back out, immediately or later, the GFCI is almost never defective itself (though it might have been misconnected [70] recently). So you will be needing to look for the cause – a ground-fault.

You should acquaint yourself with all the things that have gone dead from this tripped GFCI. These are where you will be looking for the fault. If the GFCI is in a bathroom/garage/outdoor location, outlets in all those areas may be dead. But look around, since you may not be aware of all of them. Likewise, if the device is in the kitchen/dining/nook area, see which other outlets in that area, and also outdoors, are dead and which are not affected.

The ground-fault is an unintended continuity – a touching – of either the black wire or the white wire to the ground wire or to anything grounded. Examples: a metal electrical box, other grounded metal, pipes, the earth, or things touching these. Since **this could come about within cords or appliances that are plugged into any of the dead outlets**, unplug such things and see if the GFCI will reset. If it will, plug things back in one at a time to see which one is responsible. If it won't, note whether any of the receptacles is broken, and whether they or the interiors of their boxes are wet, and whether any out in the yard receive their power by buried cable. Replace any broken ones, dry out the wet things and reset the GFCI.

If it still retrips, undo the hots and neutrals of any buried cable at the box where it seems to leave the house, and reset the GFCI. If it no longer trips, you need to reconnect and then repeat this disconnecting procedure at other boxes in the yard. If you have found nothing making contact from hot or neutral to ground or earth, then you will probably find the GFCI is still tripping for one particular piece of buried cable. So pull up, dig up, and repair or replace that piece.

If the GFCI tripped even when the line feeding out to the yard was undone, then stay indoors. Open any dead indoor boxes and look for hot *or neutral* wires making contact with any ground wires, separate them, and reset.

If no contact with ground wires was found and you have been thorough in all the procedures recommended so far, try the following procedure. Undo the hots and neutrals at a chosen point about midway among all the dead indoor items, and attempt resetting. If it retrips, the fault is upstream from that point to the GFCI. If it does not, the fault is downstream from that point. In either case, record this result, reconnect the wires, and repeat this disconnecting and resetting midway in the remaining fault area. If you keep track of which outlets and cables have been eliminated, you should be able to narrow the fault to one box or cable. You can then correct, repair, or replace as needed. You might even have banished the fault at some time in the process, by disturbing it accidentally.

19.5   Blinking or Flickering of Lights

A slight flicker or very brief dimming that corresponds to appliances turning on, or stormy weather, can be normal. But if it has become more pronounced, read on.

The flicker or dimming I am discussing here is to be distinguished from a fairly sustained dimness or brightness (lasting more than a second or two); for that see 19.9.

These blinks are due to a poor connection somewhere in your system. It is commonly at an outlet or switch box, affecting part or all of one circuit. Knowing the extent of what is affected helps identify the likely locations of the loose connection.

If one entire circuit is affected, the problem will likely be found at its breaker or its neutral connection in the panel. If several circuits in the home suffer this simultaneously, a main wire connection at the panel, main breaker, meter, or power company's line is probably compromised, and may eventually exhibit the wilder symptoms described in 19.9.

In all of these possibilities, some arcing is going on at the poor spot during the blinking. This produces a little heat or sometimes enough heat to affect the appearance of the connections or wires at that point – usually only visible when covers are removed, devices loosened, and the connections inspected. But opening many boxes in hope of seeing such signs is iffy, since there may be nothing very visible.

It can be difficult to pinpoint the source of this intermittent blink/flicker, until it has developed into a complete and final outage, which it tends to do. At that time, but also with some chance of success beforehand, the procedure in 19.7 for dealing with an open may locate the trouble spot by letting you try to produce or affect the blinking from various likely locations. Modify that procedure by noticing a production of blinks, rather than a production of good power.

19.6   Why Your Breaker Tripped But Is Holding Now

A circuit breaker tripped and you were able restore power by resetting it. Why did it trip to begin with? Were heavy loads possibly running when power was lost? A space heater, microwave oven, hair dryer, vacuum, or iron? This would have been an *overload*, That is when too much wattage being used on a circuit trips its breaker to keep the wires from getting too hot. This inconvenience is not dangerous. To avoid it, either adjust your combined use of heavy loads, find other circuits to run them from, or have a new circuit installed for such things.

Another reason a breaker could trip, but be resettable, would be that something on the circuit had a brief short circuit of some kind that is now gone. Occasionally a light bulb burning out can do this. If the circuit trips in the future, notice the circumstances.

Could your one-time tripping indicate that the breaker is going bad? Occasionally, yes, and this is almost always from a condition that leads a breaker to trip early from its own heat. This is when its internal contacts or its connection to its wire or bus bar in the panel is getting poor. If this was the cause of your tripped breaker, it will trip some day in the future and will need to be replaced. Then, locating it in a new place in the panel will insure that the false tripping is not reproduced in the new breaker by possible damage on the bus bar.

19.7   Finding an Open Hot or Open Neutral

An open is preventing part of your circuit from functioning. It is either an open neutral or an open hot. Since an open is a discontinuity, locating it can involve experimentally disturbing connections until the bad one makes good contact again briefly, or else figuring out fruitful places to look for the discontinuity.

If possible, knowing two matters will be helpful for finding the bad connection. One is whether it is the hot or the neutral that is open. The other is the extent of the outage compared to the extent of the whole circuit which has the outage happening in it.

If you do not have testers for any of the tests I will describe, you still have a good chance of locating your open using The Jiggle Method that I will also spell out.

The neutral is probably open if, at a non-working outlet, a receptacle tester reads "open neutral" or "hot and ground reversed," or if a neon or non-contact tester shows hotness [67] at either receptacle slot or at any terminal of a dead light's switch. When you know the neutral is open, you can limit the number of places to test or to look for the bad spot. This is because, with the hot still present, you can see which circuit the problem is on, by which breaker will kill that hotness. Once you know the circuit, you can further limit the parts of it you need to investigate. I will go into this soon.

On the other hand, if the hot is open, or if you have no way to determine which of the two is open, then you are in the dark about which circuit you are dealing with – unless you trust the labeling at the panel to be true and thorough. That is all right. You can still make progress.

If ten or more items are not working, you might want to go ahead and look for the open at the breakers and neutrals of your main panel itself. You would be looking for a loose, corroded, or discolored connection of the wires or be testing for hotness [67] at the breakers.

It might be that your outage extends to more than one circuit. This might be from one of the main wires having trouble at your panel, the meter, or the power company's line. However, this usually shows itself in stranger symptoms (see 19.9) than those that brought you to this part of the Diagnostic Tree.

Your first job is to know your outage better. You are very aware of the lights and outlets you used to depend on. What about the ones you never use and the ones behind furniture and stored boxes, ones you don't even remember exist? Are you going to overlook items that are unique or out of the way: the doorbell's transformer, a wired-in smoke alarm, etc.? Are any of these also not working? And notice if there are any junction boxes in areas near the outage, in case later you may need to check connections in them.

Next, if you were able to discover which breaker your outage relates to, **get equally well acquainted with the rest of that circuit**, namely, all the items of that circuit that are still working. These are "ahead of" or "upstream from" the dead outlets and lights.

Inside a home, we can usually expect an open to be located in an electrical box, rather than inside a wall or inaccessible ceiling space. It is time you should realize something now. There is a 50% chance that the open will be at the (electrically) first dead outlet, light, or switch box along the circuit. But the other 50% likelihood is that it will be found at the last *working* box before the dead ones. Therefore, you will want to keep both in mind.

Now, whether your open is of the neutral or the hot, or its type is unknown, you are going to try to disturb the bad connection back into working briefly. I call this The Jiggle Method. You may know the circuit's working things from its non-working ones, or you may have to guess that nearby working things are part of the same circuit as your non-working things. Either way, you can now get down to business.

Have all circuits turned on. Go plug a working, turned-on lamp or nightlight (or radio?) – something that will work instantly without a lag – into one of the non-working outlets. (If the outage involves no outlets, turn on the non-3-way switch of a non-fluorescent light in the outage area.) Then assign someone else the job of watching that light constantly and reporting to you immediately if it tries to light up – even the slightest flash. I suppose you could drag a light on an extension cord around with you.

Now position yourself among all the non-working items you discovered. Face toward your electrical panel. As you move in your imagination toward the panel, without regard to walls and floors, the first working items (of the circuit, if you know it) that you would start to pass among are crime suspects, along with those non-working items nearest to these working ones. Absorb this idea. Together, these two sets of items make up what I call the dead/live border. You, the detective, are to go take the covers off all outlets and switches – dead or alive – along this dead/live border [61].

Now use The Jiggle Method. Plug something else into these outlets, one after another, and wiggle it side to side somewhat. Next go back to the same outlets and also to the switches and stick a strong, thin stick of plastic or wood, not metal (e.g., chopstick) beside the device, pressing firmly on the wires you see. Then stick it further behind the device, pressing and poking various wires you can't entirely see. You can even pound on the wall near the boxes of this electrical border, and on the ceiling at light boxes. The purpose of all these activities is to disrupt wires back into good contact. If at any time your helper tells you the light flashed or stayed on, stop where you are! This is where the connection needs to be improved!

This Jiggle Method will often succeed, but certainly not always. So here is what else you can do if you have a non-contact voltage checker and you determined that your open is an open hot. Insert that tester in past the sides of each *non-working* receptacle or switch, so that it has a chance to get up against each of the wires in the box. You will probably have to loosen the device from the box somewhat to do this. If it stays lit or gives its alarm definitively, then this is where the hot has lost good contact and where you will repair it. If no non-working device shows this hot wire behind it, then it will probably be at one of the working devices you have already exposed, and you will need to visually and manually check or improve the black-wire connections at these places, with the circuit turned off.

However, if it is the neutral that is open, you will probably have to resign yourself to checking and improving the white-wire connections at both the non-working and the working places along the dead/live border.

If you never knew which kind was open, you will check and improve both black and white connections along the dead/live border. This is pictured at [61].

Another possibility. Homes built 1900-1950 may still be relying on their original knob-and-tube wiring connections. If these were not soldered well, they can be the cause of an open. They are not found in electrical boxes but in ceiling spaces and walls. If they are accessible, someone jostling them with a long stick could make the light, in the method above, flash on.

For another run at the problem, I describe this Jiggle Method a little differently at [58]. Otherwise, you may need to call in a good electrician.

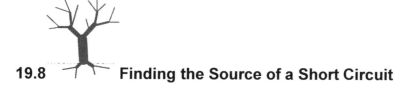

19.8   Finding the Source of a Short Circuit

A hot-to-ground short (breaker-tripping ground-fault) is more common than a hot-to-neutral short. It can be helpful to know which you have, and there is a way to know [68], but let's consider how to attack the short in any case. Most breakers can stand up to repeated shorting. Be ready to keep resetting the one in question, and keep track of which one it is. Each time, firmly click it off, then firmly push it to On. Do not be holding it on though.

First, on the dead circuit, unplug everything. Have you checked what "everything" is? Also turn all on/off switches off, and turn only one switch in each 3-4-way switch system of the circuit the other way. Try to reset. If the breaker stays on, one of those items you undid from the circuit has the short in it. So reconnect one at a time to see which one is faulty. When it involves plugging one of these items back in, I recommend having the breaker off beforehand and turning it on after inserting the plug. This avoids big sparking that you would not enjoy. The worst troubleshooting you would have to do now would be for a short in a whole bank of lights. For that, read on.

But if the breaker had retripped in spite of all the disconnections you made, then something in the permanent system is shorting – a receptacle, wire, automatic light, or hard-wired appliance, for instance. I would suspect outdoor things before indoor. In any case, pick a point along the circuit – maybe midway along – and disconnect the hots at that point. This is "divide and conquer." If the short is still there, it is electrically closer to the panel than that chosen point. If the short is gone, it is further out. By reconnecting what you undid and then opening new hots at another point in the direction of the short circuit, and by keeping track of all this, you should reach a place or a particular length of cable at which to look for the actual short.

If you suspect a recent screw or nail is to blame, see [96]. Beyond all these things, a good electrician might be needed.

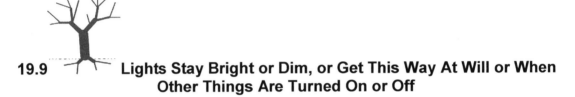

19.9   **Lights Stay Bright or Dim, or Get This Way At Will or When Other Things Are Turned On or Off**

If about half the lights of the home are dead or dim, most likely a main hot wire is open – at the panel, main breaker, meter, or the power company's line. Often, the dead lights may begin to run dimly when a 240-volt appliance is run. I have found the source of these main opens to be more often outdoors in the power company's domain, so I recommend they be called. If, instead, this might be occurring in your panel, see [38].

If at times some lights run dimly and others brightly, for several seconds or even minutes at a time, this is an open neutral. If most of the home is affected in this way, it is probably the main neutral that is open. The source of this would be located at your panel, the meter area, or more often the power company's line. For a main neutral problem, I recommend you call the power company before any electrician. Damage to electronic items in your home is probably occurring.

However, if these open neutral symptoms are limited to one or two circuits, then the open neutral is probably one that is shared by two circuits [36]. In that case, the poor connection will be in one of two places. The easier one to check is these two circuits' neutral in the panel. If you identify the breaker for the most affected circuit, its partner circuit will be the one leaving the panel in the same cable. The other place to check is the first box these two circuits go to from the panel. This box will contain a red wire and will usually be located toward the panel-end of the areas served by the two circuits. Damage can likewise occur to items running on these two circuits during the problem.

19.10   One Item Out

You have identified your electrical outage as limited (are you sure?) to one thing or to one set of lights controlled by the same switch. For a light, replace bulbs you assume are good with ones you know work. See if the fixture itself is discolored, with sockets cracking from past heat. For an outlet, plug something else in than what made you think the outlet was dead. For an appliance or other item that plugs into outlets, try running it out of a working outlet; you can move the item or run an extension cord to it. If these activities haven't changed your mind about what is wrong, you may find replacing any of the trouble-things – including a fixture, switch, or receptacle – solves the problem. If not, go to the Open at 19.7.

19.11   Electric Heat Problems

Most permanent electric heaters run on 240 volt circuits, and this is what will be dealt with here. But if you know your heater uses 120 volts, treat its problem as if the heater were a light and the thermostat were a switch. There could even be lights and outlets on the same circuit. In other words, go to the start of this Diagnostic Tree [80], treating the problem as a light or outlet problem.

Before we consider individual room heaters, **a word on central electric furnace problems**. Many furnace troubles will be internal to it – not in the scope of this guide. The problems having to do with furnace circuits will tend show up as one tripping double breaker (out of as many as three the furnace might have at the panel), or a tripping breaker in the front of the furnace itself, or the furnace not running or not running on full heat. These symptoms can easily be from wires or contacts overheating at the breakers of the panel or of the furnace. Inspecting around those breakers will tend to show damage from such heat. Replacement and perhaps other repair would then be needed. These areas are so subject to overheating because the high current that runs through these breakers is less tolerant of poor connections than lighter current is.

Room (zonal) electric heaters are usually either fan-forced in-wall heaters or the long baseboard radiators. They are run on circuits dedicated to heat or air conditioning only. A circuit can often have more than one heater and serve more than one room. Many in-wall heaters now have a reset button (red or not), which keeps the individual heater from functioning once it has overheated its interior. Once this button is found behind the grill, pushing it in firmly may let the heater work again. But the popping off may have been due to an unsafe condition that will recur unless addressed. This might be dust accumulation, worn fan bearings, or the wrong grill.

Room heaters have elements that can burn out. Other components can fail too. When a part fails, replacement of the entire heater is often easier than finding the proper new part.

But sometimes the failure of a heater to run is from something else that is repairable or replaceable. This could be a bad thermostat or breaker, or a wire connection that has gone bad somewhere. These would be the case if more than one heater is controlled by a thermostat and they all stop working at once, or if more than one room's heaters stop at the same time. It could also be the case with just one room or one heater. The places to look for poor connectors include: that circuit's breaker, its thermostat boxes, and where the cable for the heater(s) in question enters it or leaves another heater that is working. Poor connections can involve black wires, but also white ones – which, with electric heat, are also hot wires, not neutrals.

Zonal heat provides **thermostatic control for each heated area**. Typically, these thermostats are factory calibrated so that the temperature settings stated on them correspond to the actual temperature they will maintain in the room. There will still be a lag of two or three degrees as the heater continues heating before its heat has had a chance to affect the thermostat. People not familiar with such small but noticeable "swings" sometimes try to compensate for this by turning the thermostat way up or down, thinking the extreme settings will make things happen faster. They won't.

There are two ways that a thermostat can be inaccurate. One is that its calibration from the factory, or over time, has become five or even ten degrees off from the truth. Many have a small setscrew – painted in place so it won't move – that can readjust the calibration (judged by where the clicking sound occurs around the dial). However, many people are happy to ignore the strict temperatures stated on the thermostat and simply remember a setting that feels comfortable to them, perhaps marking this with a pencil.

The other inaccuracy of a thermostat is more extreme. This would be when its control of heat is either wildly erratic or occurs, if at all, only at the very low end of the scale – the room definitely overheats. This tends to mean the thermostat is on its death bed, internally stuck on, even when the dial is turned down. Also see [110].

Some large room areas use a low-voltage thermostat in conjunction with a relay. Calibration and "swing" problems for these can usually be addressed at the thermostat, whereas complete loss of control will mean the relay is bad. Good luck finding and recognizing the relay, which looks partly like a doorbell transformer.

There is one further rare condition that can result in 240-volt zone heat running despite a thermostat being turned down. When the element of a heater shorts to the metal frame or fins near it, it can run constantly at a low wattage and not trip the breaker. The heat produced will be at 25% of the usual output – just warm to the touch.

19.12   Finding the Source of a Shock

Caution: Please do not continue using your body to judge whether stray voltage is still there. I recommend a neon tester, with one probe held to the palm of your hand, to check metal for hotness [67]. A non-contact voltage checker may pick up false indications of shock hazard. For safety, turn the circuit off when changing things on the circuit and only back on for testing the result.

For this sort of ground-fault, **two strategies are possible**. One is to leave the ungrounded fault in place and locate it first, grounding things better later. The other is to provide a good ground to the thing that delivered the shock. This will probably create a breaker-tripping short, and then you can deal with it as a Short at 19.8. Though it feels less safe and I have to be more careful about myself, I find it more efficient to use the first strategy. You should attempt what is safe in your judgment, according to your knowledge.

If you have decided to leave the hot things hot, first see which circuit, when turned off, eliminates the hotness. Get well acquainted with all the other things that are part of that circuit. Then turn it back on. See if those other things show that stray hotness, including the grounding hole of receptacles. If the home was built after the 1960s, hotness is more likely to be limited to one thing or to the fraction of the circuit from which a ground wire has become disconnected. If the home was built before the 1960s, it is likely to spread hotness to various metal things if metal-sheathed cable has lost its contact with ground.

If nothing else shows hotness, disconnect the hot wire of the shocking item. If hotness disappears from the shocking metal of that item, then it has the faulting wire or part within it. If hotness persists, then on this circuit unplug everything, and turn all on/off switches off, and turn only one switch in each 3- or 4-way system the other way. Did one of these actions eliminate the hotness? If so, that item or set of lights is harboring the short.

Look along this circuit for any broken receptacles, like where a too-long silver cover-screw may have broken the receptacle's plastic apart. Also, take all covers off receptacles and switches of the circuit, and look for a ground wire curled up next to the hot terminals.

If the shock – the hotness – is not always there, is there some automatic appliance or light that is responsible when it turns on – at certain times of the day, for instance.

Beyond all this, **pick a point midway along the circuit and undo its hot wires there**. If the shock-location hotness disappears, then the fault was coming from somewhere electrically beyond (away from panel) this point of the circuit. If the shock-place is still hot, the fault is electrically back toward the panel from here. You can reconnect the hots and then repeat this divide-and-conquer procedure at other points to narrow the fault location down. To avoid confusion, record your results as you go.

If nothing leads you to the fault, you can give a good ground to the shocking thing, so that a short is created and perhaps trips the breaker. Then troubleshoot it as a Short at 19.8.

CHAPTER 20

Frequently Answered Questions

Home electrical problems raise common questions that may be answered here. The categories listed below are all geared to solving malfunctions and miswirings in your electrical system, not design or installation concerns. There are several questions in most of these alphabetized categories:

Basic House Wiring Knowledge
Basic Knowledge About Electrical Circuits
Circuit Breakers
Diagrams
Electrical Code
Electrical Noises or Sparks
Finding a Ground-Fault
Finding a Loose Connection
Finding the Source of Short Circuit
Fire Dangers
GFCIs
High Utility Bills
Light Bulbs
Odd Lighting Behavior
Outages
Outdoor Wiring Problems
Overloads
Repairs
Replacing Outlets and Switches
Shocks
Smells or Heat Noticed
Switches
Terms and Definitions
Testing

Basic House Wiring Knowledge

Which wires are supposed to attach where on a receptacle (outlet)? As you look at the face of the receptacle with its slots above its hole, the shorter slot on the right gets the hot wires by attachment on that side. The longer slot on the left gets the neutral (white) wires by attachment on that side. The hole gets the (bare/green) ground wire by attachment to the green screw. See [12].

Which wires of a light fixture are supposed to connect to the black, the white, and the bare (or green) wire at the light box? If there is a bare or green wire in the box, attach the fixture's bare or green (if any) to it, otherwise leave the fixture's alone. If the other wires of the fixture are black and white, connect them each to the same color wire in the box. But if a single red is waiting in the box, attaching the fixture's black to it and not to the blacks in the box, is probably the right move. If the fixture's two non-ground wires are not black and white but one of them is smooth and the other has a "ribbed" texture, the ribbed one is to connect to the white of the box and the smooth one to the switched hot. But if the fixture's wires fit none of these descriptions, one of the two should be a solid color (it connects to the switched hot; except if it is solid white, connect it to the white) and the other should have striping or lettering on it (it goes to the white neutral; except, if its mate was solid white, this striped one goes to the switched hot). Is everything clear? These standards must have come from the IRS. I don't know them by heart.

Can you help me understand how a circuit in my home operates? For this I refer you to the Background Chapters (2-11) and also to the Typical Circuit [18].

Is there a way to map out the circuits in my home? A thorough mapping would mean you know what box every part of the circuit branches out from. But maybe you just need to know all the things running off each separate circuit breaker. It can take some work. Chapter 10 [44] is about how to go about labeling your panel.

What goes wrong with circuits? You can lose power or part of your power. Your automatic breakers or GFCIs can switch things off. Your lights can flicker or get bright or strangely dim. To understand why such things happen, see Chapter 3 [14].

How can I turn off all my power so I can be safe checking or working on my wiring? There may be a single main shut-off breaker in your main panelbox or somewhere close by, indoors or outside. Or it may be you will need to turn off as many as six different breakers or levers. If unsure, turning off all breakers and pulling out all fuses you are aware of – indoors and out – should work, but a tester that will confirm that "hotness" is gone [67].

What is meant by pigtailing? Pigtailing is combining two or more wires with an additional wire which will be the one to attach to a terminal or fixture. Screw terminals that clamp down on wires you insert in nearby holes often let you connect more than one wire there, so that there is no need to pigtail. But more often the screws only take wires curled clockwise directly under themselves. Only one wire should be put under each screw. So it may be necessary to pigtail so that all the (say, white) wires of the circuit connecting there have contact with each other. On some devices there are (additional) holes for terminating wires by simply pushing wires in till they catch. If there are enough such holes, pigtailing will not be needed. Such holes on receptacles will not accept large (12 gauge) wires, in which case the wires will need to be pigtailed if there are not enough screws to put them all under. See the drawing at [17].

Can I tell if my home is wired safely? Honestly, no. Not even an inspector or electrician can. Some things are hidden from view and from testing. An investigation that tried to be as thorough as possible would still fall short. Even when something loose or against Code is discovered, the degree of hazard it presents is disputable. Most "potentially unsafe" conditions will show themselves as outages, flickerings, shorts, or shocks. When they do, most prove themselves to be minor or contained. I am not saying an inspection and someone's opinion of the results are pointless or of no value. But because people can make money off your anxieties, the truth about your risk and about their thoroughness can get exaggerated. See [115].

Basic Knowledge About Electrical Circuits

What is electricity? Well, tame electricity (not static electricity or lightning) is essentially a force generated onto loops of conductive material, transferred through their electrons, and applied as useful energy at parts of these loops.

What is meant by a circuit? A circuit is the actual or intended path of current between points of differing voltage. In the case of a household 120 volt circuit, the path is through a "hot" wire from the breaker, an item that is using the electricity, and a "neutral" wire connected to the grounded neutral bar in the panel. In a sense, each loop that current makes (through a single light and its switch, for instance) is a circuit. But the most common meaning is the "branch circuit," that is, everything fed (or interrupted) by a given breaker or fuse. See [10].

To avoid getting shocked if I work on my system, do I need to turn off all power to the home? It's not a bad idea. If you know enough about your system to turn less off at once, you may be safe turning a single breaker off or just a GFCI or switch. It is also a good habit to treat all wires as live anyway, even when you have checked and know they are dead. You don't know everything, and you don't have control of people in the home who might forget about you and turn something back on. Including yourself. See [5].

Circuit Breaker Questions

Does a circuit breaker go bad or get weak? It doesn't start tripping at a lower level than it should, unless a loose connection/contact in/under/at it is making heat that throws it off. Cases where the handle of the breaker mechanically will not reset are rare. It is more common that failure to reset is from a short circuit [56] that retrips it immediately or from the person not knowing the right procedure [62] for resetting. Of all home circuit problems, breakers get a lot of suspicion. Only a fraction of it is deserved.

How can I tell if a circuit breaker is bad? In general see [66]. You can replace it or move its wire, temporarily, to another breaker. If this doesn't improve things, the old breaker is fine. Look for another cause than the breaker. For instance, an open [58].

Diagrams

Do you have a diagram of how switches or outlets are usually hooked up? Yes, several, especially the Typical Circuit [18].

Do you have a diagram of how cables are usually run in a home? Yes, at [23]. It reflects the same relation of switches and outlets shown in the Typical Circuit [21]. There are common methods of wiring a house or apartment, but not quite a "usual" way.

Do you have a diagram of a main electrical panel box or how a 240-volt circuit is hooked up? Yes, at [9].

Electrical Code

Why do some circuits seem to go all over the place without obvious reason? There are many Code provisions saying where some circuits may not extend, where they must be provided; where switches, fixtures, and receptacles must and may not be. But residential Code and blueprints do not say everything about how circuits should run. Within Code, electricians will then choose convenient and material-saving routes for the cables.

How many things can be on a circuit; how many wired from a GFCI? For a general purpose circuit, the limitation is mainly this: a 15-amp circuit should not extend over more than 600 sq. ft. of the home; a 20-amp circuit not over 800 sq. ft. There is usually no further limit to the number of outlets that can be wired as load from a GFCI. It is reported that a very lengthy set of GFCI loads might set up enough capacitance to trip the GFCI. If that is suspected, each such load outlet could be given its own GFCI device, connected to protect only itself [31].

When were different things required by Code? That's a large question that I don't get into, except for GFCI requirements [71].

Electrical Noises or Sparks

Why is my light, switch, or breaker box humming? Many dimmer switches will set up a hum at the light bulbs. At the breaker panel, the 60 cycles per second of your alternating current is able to set up a vibration or slight buzz or hum in some components there. Fluorescent lights, transformers, and an electric water heater can be heard humming also. All these are fairly normal, but if a hum is quite loud, it may mean a component is loose or close to failing. I have come across wet circuit breakers buzzing as they boil their water. In another case, a loud hum was a breaker carrying a significant overload without tripping as it should have.

Why does my breaker hum or spark and then turn off? If it makes this noise as soon as it is turned on and then trips off quickly or within ten seconds, there is a short circuit [56] occurring somewhere out on the circuit. If sparking or "fizzling" is heard or seen but the breaker doesn't go off until a minute or more has elapsed, the breaker itself is having a connection problem and will probably need to be replaced.

Finding a Ground-fault

Since my GFCI keeps tripping, where do I look for the ground-fault? This will be similar to finding a short circuit (below) with the additional aspect that the fault to ground can come from the hot or from the neutral. Look among the things that have gone dead. See [57].

How can I find what is tripping the GFCI if it only happens once in awhile? On this question, I share your pain. I haven't tried it much, but theoretically an ohmmeter might show a non-infinite resistance of over 30k ohms between ground and either hot or neutral, when you test (with power off) at any fully disconnected point downstream from the GFCI. This resistance won't have been enough to trip the GFCI but may be enough to track down the fault. Unfortunately we can sometimes get a similar reading across wires that are virtually separate. Also this idea won't help much if the fault is to the earth alone, not to the ground wire. If you learn that Code does not require GFCI protection for your load, you could consider hooking the load up to normal power instead.

Finding a Loose Connection

I've narrowed my outage down to a loose hot or neutral somewhere; can I find the spot without tearing everything apart? Maybe. For details on how to narrow the spot down see [58].

I've checked, tightened, or replaced all my dead outlets and switches, and they're still dead. Now what? Have you considered that the bad connection can be at a nearby *working* outlet or switch as easily as at a dead one? There may be odd places you haven't checked – another room (downstairs?), a smoke alarm box or a doorbell transformer box in a closet.

Finding the Source of a Short Circuit

A breaker retrips when I reset it. If it is a short, where should I look? If it is truly retripping, not having a rare mechanical problem, and if you are attempting the reset correctly [62], then it is a short. On that circuit, unplug everything and turn all simple switches off, and turn one end of any three-way switches the other way. If the short recurs upon resetting, see next question.

To find my short I turned off all the switches and unplugged everything of the circuit. Why is it still shorting? The short is in a more permanent part of the wiring (in a box, receptacle, or wire). See [56]. Have you made sure you know the extent of the circuit (outdoors, closets, attic, crawl space)?

I suspect that recent screws or nails hit a wire. Can I tell which screw? If you are able (at the panel, for instance) to unconnect the neutral and ground wires and keep them isolated from anything grounded, then when the breaker is reset, it may not trip. If it does not trip, your ground and/or neutral wires will probably register hot, as will the theorized nail or screw and many appliances on the circuit! So put people out of the house before doing this! A non-contact voltage tester would then indicate pretty well which of all the screws is live. If you can touch its head with a neon tester (in hand), it will confirm the culprit. Extracting it might leave the cable functional and safe, but you could bare the structure to be sure or to make a definite repair.

Fire Dangers

To be safe, should I have my whole electrical system checked out, and how often? Without any definite specific symptoms, there is no reason to have things checked more than once, if that, during your tenure at a home, unless you enjoy being paranoid. And don't let anyone confuse you between technical Code violations and active hazards.

How likely is an electrical fire? The question is unclear. You can see my thoughts on this at [115].

GFCI-GFI Questions

What is a GFCI for? A GFCI receptacle or a GFCI breaker is to prevent fatal shocks at likely locations – where people operating faulty tools or appliances can easily become a good path to ground, completing an unintended circuit.

Is there a difference between a GFCI and a GFI? GFCI stands for "ground-fault circuit interrupter." GFI stands for "ground-fault interrupter." They are the same thing. I prefer "GFI" because the word "circuit" is unnecessary and confusing.

How does a GFCI work? By "work" here you mean how does it know to trip off. A GFCI trips off (stopping power at itself and often other outlets) by comparing how much current is flowing on its hot versus its neutral wires. It trips if these are different by a small fraction of one amp, which would be the result of someone being shocked (giving current an alternate path than just between hot and neutral). But other unbalanced current conditions are able to trip these devices besides someone being shocked.

Why won't my GFCI reset? There are several possibilities. It may be responding to a ground-fault happening somewhere downstream, at regular outlets that are now dead, for instance. It could be the GFCI itself has no power reaching its electrical box because of a short or an open or another GFCI that is tripped upstream from it. Tripped GFCIs made since 2002 will not let you reset them if power is not getting to them. See [70].

Does a GFCI go bad, and how can I tell? The main way a GFCI truly is bad is if it still runs things after you push the test button. In that case, it is not protecting anyone from fatal shock, at itself or at other outlets it was protecting. The idea that a GFCI is bad because it won't reset is almost always wrong. GFCIs made since 2002 won't reset if they are not receiving good power in the first place. And a GFCI made before 2002, whose reset stays in, can fail to run things for the same reason – not receiving good power itself. In other cases a GFCI "not resetting" is just retripping for some kind of ground-fault. This is not a case of the "GFCI going bad" either. It calls for correcting a fault condition downstream from the GFCI. Only once or twice have I seen a GFCI trip or fail to reset from a mechanical problem in it. See [70].

If my GFCI won't reset, should I replace it? You could, but it is much more common for a GFCI receptacle to retrip (or to not reset) for other reasons than a bad GFCI. Your new GFCI would probably not reset either. I wouldn't suspect the GFCI itself until I had ruled out the more usual causes. Here they are. There could be a ground-fault happening at some "downstream" wire or receptacle or item plugged in there. Your GFCI that won't reset could have been installed incorrectly recently; since 2002 GFCI receptacles have had a feature that won't let them reset if they are hooked up wrong or if power is not on. See [31] and [70].

High Utility Bills

Why has my electric power bill been so high lately? First, think of whether you have been using more. A portable heater? De-icing equipment? I know of no wiring condition that would be capable of running up a high bill. However, if your water is heated electrically, a leaking hot water pipe would definitely explain a high bill. I have also heard of defective refrigerators running inefficiently and therefore constantly. Yes, you can also see if the power company is willing to check or replace their meter.

Light Bulbs

Why do the bulbs of a certain fixture burn out a lot? When a fixture cannot dissipate the heat of its bulbs, it takes a toll on the bulbs and on the fixture's sockets and wires. If the lights are ones that are left on a lot – like outdoor lights left on all night – then the bulbs may be living their full life but will simply have to be changed more often than others. Other things can contribute to early failure. Bulbs may be of cheap quality, or there may be loose arcing connections at the socket or in connections to the light.

Why do many bulbs around the house burn out sooner than they should? There are various reasons that bulbs will burn out too soon. Bulbs may be of cheap quality, or there may be loose arcing connections in the wiring of a circuit. The life expectancy of a bulb will also be affected by the quality of power from the power company. This includes the little surges and spikes that are better known for their effect on computers. But it also includes the basic voltage level coming to the home from the utility. Many homes receive more than the average 120 volts that most bulbs are designed to handle and this shortens their stated life. A good solution to this is to look for the same bulb but with a "130v" rating stamped on the bulb instead of "120v." The light output of these won't be quite as bright, but you will spend less of your time getting the ladder or stool out again.

Several bulbs (got real bright and) burned out about the same time. You may have a loose neutral that is shared by two circuits [36] and allows high voltage to hit one of the circuits. Or the poor neutral could be the main neutral [38].

Odd Lighting Behavior

What causes my lights to flicker? This comes from a poor connection or contact somewhere along the circuit, or even at a main wire outdoors or in the panel. See [84].

Some lights dim down for a time, others get extra bright; what's going on? A shared neutral wire – sometimes the main one at the panel or outside from the power company – is having trouble. Repair is more likely to be a job for the power company than for an electrician or yourself. See [38] and [36].

I turn an appliance on and it makes lights that were dead come on; what's happening? A main hot wire is having trouble at the panel or outside. The power company is often responsible, so call them first. Otherwise or later, an electrician. To understand what is going on see [38].

Outages

How can a circuit go out with no breaker or GFCI tripped? In a word, by a connection being bad somewhere. The whole circuit would fail to work if a connection-point at the breaker or at the circuit's neutral in the panel became loose or deteriorated. More often these "opens" involve less than the entire circuit. A connection out on the circuit – at an outlet box for instance – has failed.

Some things are not working; how can I know where to look for the problem? If you have checked bulbs and generator switches, and have reset any breakers and GFCIs, you will probably need to look for an open (loose, corroded, broken) connection. But start at [81].

Some things will go out for awhile and later come back on (on their own); what is that? That is a poor connection being poorer sometimes and better at other times. It will be generating some heat at the poor spot whenever it does run things. It will tend to progress toward staying out and never coming back on. See [82].

Why would a neutral wire read live? When a white wire is not continuous back to the panel as it should be, the hotness of the hot wire still goes through anything that is ready to run (but won't) and shows up on this normally-neutral wire.

Outdoor Wiring Problems

How can I tell if a short, ground-fault, or open outdoors is in the earth or at a fixture/outlet? If you can get access to all connection points of this line, you can unconnect just fixtures and outlets from the line and see if the fault remains when you try to reset. Otherwise, unconnecting where you can will often let you narrow the possibilities down in a divide-and-conquer fashion. See [87] and [83]. An open [85] in the yard is likelier to be at a connection above ground, where wires don't end up shorting so easily.

Overloads

How can I tell if I am overloading a circuit? Most easily by letting the breaker trip and then recall what all was running that now is dead. If the breaker doesn't trip, you are not overloading. Are you "overloading" a receptacle, surge strip, or extension cord by the number of things you have plugged in? Not likely, although you should check the tag on the extension cord for the most watts you should have running on it. Even when these things are within their limits, any cord or receptacle can get hotter than it should because of a defect in or damage to it. If you notice extreme heat, replacement is important. Dimmers are a different story [105].

The breaker often trips when I am using the vacuum (or hair dryer or iron); is that normal and what can I do? It is almost normal, since the manufacturers of vacuums and hair dryers have increased the percentage of a circuit's capacity their appliances use. If it is too inconvenient to live with this problem, a new circuit to an outlet, just for such a heavy user, will do the trick. If a hair dryer has a low setting, using that will help.

Repairs

Am I allowed to make a splice in the breaker panel? Yes. It would have to be 75% full of wires for the answer to be No.

Why would a new breaker go bad after a while, like the old one did? Because the way the old one went bad was by bad contact with the bus bar, so that arcing there damaged the bus bar. Put *another* new breaker in, but in a better place.

What is the best way to connect wires at a receptacle? By pigtailing [93], if you do a good job of it. Second choice: wires wrapped clockwise under side-screws. Third choice: use a receptacle whose side-screws clamp the wires tight in holes. Last choice (and only for 14 gauge wire): the "quick wire" push-in holes on the back of the receptacle; this actually does OK most of the time and is the most common.

Replacing Outlets and Switches

Will it be easy for me to replace switches and outlets in my home? Physically, maybe. Electrically, maybe not. For many people, the unknowns they will encounter when they get into this simple sounding project will begin to baffle them. If they go forward anyway, they are likely to end up with one or more malfunctions when they turn power back on and try using things. If they are lucky and everything seems to check out fine, their inexperience at making the new connections may still result in problems in the future. See [41].

I replaced several receptacles or switches with new ones; things don't work quite right now; what did I do? You'll need to go back over the work you did and see if all connections are solid, none missing, and whether something was connected incorrectly. See [41].

I am replacing old switches or outlets but have maybe lost track of how they were connected; is there a standard way or diagram? Without consulting an electrician, your best bet is the examples in the Typical Circuit [21].

What is the green screw on my new switch for? People have been replacing plastic switch covers with decorative metal ones. So Code has now required switches to be grounded, so that the covers attached to them will never be able to shock if a hot wire were to get loose and touch either. So to put the new switch in correctly in a plastic box, you'll dig the bundle of ground wires out from the back of the box and pigtail [93] one bare wire from them to this green screw.

Shocks

I get shocked when touching two things at once but not either alone; which one has the problem? Without a tester, the only way to tell is to touch a third thing from each, at some risk to your health! So I recommend a neon tester or a non-contact tester; they will tend to show which one is live. See [58].

We get shocked off faucets or pipes sometimes; what can we do? The particular circuit responsible can be identified and the stray wire or point of contact located. See [58]. Plus, the grounding of those pipes should be checked and assured. Rarely, if you live close to some big main lines of your power company, those lines might be able to create voltage on your pipes. The power company might be able to help.

Smells or Heat Noticed

Should I be concerned that a certain switch or outlet gets physically hot? An outlet's getting hot means that wires connecting to it are loose and need help or that the outlet needs to be replaced because its receivers, that a cord plugs into, are weak. You need to repair either of these scenarios. A hot switch is usually a dimmer switch. It may or may not still be able to dim lights. If the dimmer is controlling more than 600 watts worth of light bulbs, it is probably overloaded. In that case, install one rated to handle more watts, or replace bulbs with lower-watt ones, or replace the dimmer with a regular switch.

Why is a circuit breaker so hot? Breakers will be mildly warm when running things, but if one is hotter (not necessarily too hot to touch) it might be having trouble with a poor connection at or in it. Consider what it is running. If a heavy load (a space heater, for instance) has been running for perhaps a solid hour, this would be normal, and the breaker might be about to trip from the heat.

I've smelled something funny like hot plastic; what might be happening? It isn't always easy to pinpoint where smells are coming from, but try. It might not be from an electrical source, but it might be. Sniff up close to outlets and switches when you notice the smell. Has a pet of yours taken "nose interest" in a certain area? If the smell is from something electrical, it will be from a poor connection (or occasionally a poor short) that is creating heat and melting or charring plastic components. This presents a possible fire hazard.

Switch Questions

Why are switches called 3-way when there are only two switches? Only because there are three terminals on the switch mechanism, which isn't a good reason in my opinion. It is true, however, that the switches used to switch lights from multiple locations are not all the same type of switch. Two of them have the three terminals, but any additional locations beyond the two have to use switches with four terminals, called 4-way. To be even more technical, a 3-way switch is a single-pole double-throw switch, and a 4-way switch is a double-pole double throw switch arranged for pole-reversing. See [24].

We replaced some switches and now the new ones don't work quite right. Why? You probably hooked the new ones up incorrectly. If the switches involved were 3- or 4-way type, the new switches may have a different arrangement of terminals than the old ones did. If the switches involved were normal on-off (single pole) type and there were more than two wires to attach, you may have attached a wrong wire somewhere or you may have failed to attach one at all, since the switch only seemed to call for two. See [42].

I lost track of how the wires were connected to the old switch. How can I know what to do without trying dozens of possibilities? For this you need to learn more about how wires relate to switches. See the Typical Circuit [18].

Can you help me hook up a 4-way switch right? Yes, I can at least advise you so your choices and experimentation are minimized. Two of the switch's terminal screws are one color (brassy?) and the other two another color (dark?). Of all the wires in the switch box, two that come from one cable as it enters the box will attach to the two screws of one color, and two wires that come from the other cable (I hope there are just two cables total) will attach to the screws of the other color. If there are more than two insulated wires in both of those cables, the third wires of each cable would attach to each other, not to the switch. Hopefully these "third" wires were identified by already being joined, so that you don't have to experiment to find out which of the three wires in a cable is this "third" one. Colors can vary. See [24].

Terms and Definitions

What is the difference between hot, neutral, and ground wires? When connected properly, these wires serve different functions, as follows. Hot ("live") wires provide a circuit's path between the breaker and any lights or appliances. Neutral wires provide the rest of the path, that is, the path between these same lights or appliances and the panel's grounded neutral bar. The ground wires are connected, like the neutrals, to the grounding point in the panel, but they are not supposed to carry current under normal conditions. In an abnormal condition like the hot shorting to metal parts nearby, the ground wire is meant (by its attachment to such metal) to carry a great amount of current suddenly, so as to trip the hot's breaker and so to isolate the condition. See [11].

What is the difference between open, overload, short, ground-fault? An open is when a circuit's path is disrupted. An overload is when current used on a circuit is a bit excessive. A short is when current takes an unintended path to ground, usually with very little resistance. A ground-fault is when such a short does not use the neutral as its path to ground. See [15].

What does open ground mean? open neutral? reverse polarity, etc.? Measured at an outlet's receptacle, the path (wire continuity) to the ground point in the panel can be disrupted or missing for the ground wire (open ground) or for the neutral (open neutral). When it is the path between the outlet and its circuit breaker that is disrupted, this is an open hot. Reverse polarity (hot and neutral reversed) means neutral wires are connected to the side of the receptacle that is supposed to be for the hots, and vice versa. See [73].

What is the difference between current, voltage, resistance, and wattage? Voltage pushes current through a resistance, using power (wattage). See [130].

What is the difference between amperes, ohms, watts, and volts? W volts push X amperes through Y ohms, using Z watts. Amps times ohms = volts. Amps times volts = watts. See [130].

What is the difference between outlet, receptacle, switch, and breaker? A switch makes or breaks continuity. A breaker is a switch that automatically breaks continuity when current is too high. An outlet is technically where a light or appliance gets its connection to the circuit's wires. A receptacle is the device we often call "outlet," for plugging cords into. See [130].

What is the difference between fixture, device, and appliance? A fixture is a non-portable light. An appliance is anything other than a light that uses wattage. A device (e.g., switch, breaker, receptacle) is for passing or purposely disrupting the continuity of the circuit to fixtures, appliances, or lamps. See [130].

Testing

What is the right tester to use for my problem? See [46].

What does this 3-prong outlet tester mean by an open ground, open neutral, reverse polarity, or "hot and ground reversed"? See [73], [63], and [102] above.

How would I test for a good or bad neutral, hot, or ground? The best all-around is a neon tester. With one probe in the palm or your hand and the other to a possible hot, it glows for a hot. With one probe to the hot, it glows even brighter when the other is to a good neutral or ground. But see [65].

How would I test for a good or bad switch, receptacle, GFCI, breaker, or fuse? If a hooked up non-dimmer non-3way *switch* shows hot at one terminal (neon tester in hand) but not at the other when the switch is turned to On, the switch is bad. Or just join the switch's two wires; if the light works but didn't for the switch, the switch is bad. A *receptacle* may need replacing but that will be from not holding plugs well, or from it having overheated from a poor wire connection, or from being simply broken. If a *GFCI* that can run things won't trip off for the test button, replace it. And if a GFCI with good hot and neutral at its line terminals won't reset and run things when no load wires are connected, replace it. (I have seen this only once.) Other than these, the GFCI itself is good. A *breaker*'s screw showing hot for your neon tester is good 95% of the time. If moving a breaker's wire to another breaker changes nothing in the circuit's behavior, the breaker was fine. A screwed-in *fuse,* lighting a one-probe-in-hand neon tester touched to its outer threads, is good; if it doesn't light, the fuse is bad *if* it lights on the fuseholder's center when the fuse is removed. A cartridge fuse that can be probed while in place is good if both ends are hot and neon probes to both ends at once make no light; if probes to both ends at once give light, it is bad. If fuses must be pulled out to test, an ohmmeter showing 0-5 ohms means good, otherwise maybe bad. Generally see [65].

At not-working outlets I find full voltage between hot and ground but not hot to neutral. Why? The neutral is open somewhere. See [74].

The white neutrals at some dead items of my circuit register some voltage to ground. Why? Something among the not-working items of the circuit is turned on, allowing hotness from the good hot wire to go through the light bulb filament, say, and show up as somewhat hot where you are testing the white wires, which are open.

I get a reading on my voltmeter or ohmmeter that I don't understand. Am I testing the right things? Maybe not. There are a lot more readings that are hard to explain than those that make sense and tell you what you need to know. I don't test anything but what I know will probably give me usable information. When I don't understand a reading, I don't let it distract me. I think of a different way to test out what I need to know. Knowing whether, what, and where to test is worth some thought. See [48].

My non-contact volt "stick" says something is hot or dead, but other testers disagree. What's up? A non-contact voltage-presence indicator is rated to say when a certain (or greater) level of voltage is present. In practice I have found that that level is elastic. Lower voltages can set it off at times, especially when placing the stick very close to a wire. Also, voltage induced onto a wire from nearby hot wires can register [65]. So it is often helpful to confirm what a stick says using other testers and to give the others higher credibility. See the chart of testers [46]. hot underground cables that are still close to the earth may not register hotness for a stick.

CHAPTER 21

Problems With Particular Electrical Items

This chapter focuses on some particular devices and appliances that may need special troubleshooting because of their unique features. In alphabetical order, they are:

Arc-Fault Interrupters (AFCIs)
Dimmers
Disposals
Doorbells
Dryers
Generator Switches
Hair Dryers
Hot Tubs
Light Bulbs
Microwave Ovens
Motion Sensors
Photocells
Ranges
Receptacles
Smoke Alarms
Space Heaters
Switched Outlets
Thermostats
Timers
Two-Hole Receptacles
Water Heaters
X-10 Switching

Arc-Fault Interrupters (AFCIs)

New with the 2002 Code, these special circuit breakers with an extra button are able to identify and trip for a kind of arcing [130] at cords, outlets and lights, that has caused some fires. As of 2007, they have only been required for circuits to bedrooms. Most AFCIs are made with GFCI-type protection built into them as well. So these AFCIs are liable to complicate the troubleshooting process. The tripping of a normal breaker already presents us with several possibilities: short, overload, or the breaker's connections overheating. An AFCI could trip for these same things plus for a ground-fault or an arc-fault. As long as it keeps tripping for the troubleshooter, which cause is at work and where it is happening will be possible to determine by different procedures [50]. But if it repeats its tripping only once in awhile, good luck.

Dimmer Switches

A dimmer saves some electricity and bulb-life. Dimmers normally produce some heat when operating. A rule of thumb is that if you can keep your thumb on the cover-plate screw without getting burned, this is normal. Unless rated to handle more, a dimmer controlling more than 600 watts of lighting will get hotter than it is designed for, and will not last long. Most dimmers have electronic components that are vulnerable to surges. Specially rated dimmers are needed for low voltage lights. None are meant for normal fluorescent bulbs/tubes/fixtures.

Disposals

A garbage disposal is usually given its own circuit. Occasionally it may share with a trash compactor or dishwasher, or, in older homes, with a nearby kitchen outlet circuit. A disposal that runs all the time regardless of its switch may have been plugged into the wrong half of a double receptacle under the sink. A disposal that hums when turned on, but doesn't turn, is probably jammed. If it doesn't hum or turn, the breaker could be tripped or a (red) button on the disposal may need to be pushed to reset it. Such tripping was to protect the motor from overheating, from a jam perhaps.

Doorbells

The most common doorbell system in homes runs on 12-16 volts and consists of a pushbutton, a transformer, and the chime itself. These are wired in relation to one another with 18 to 22 gauge bellwire, thermostat cable, or phone cable. Only two wires are usually needed between these components. In the 1940s through 1960s it was common for the chime to ring differently for front and back doors, and so two pushbuttons were wired. More recently electronic chimes have become available. They may need a stronger transformer and/or more wires. Among problems a chime can have are a sticky chime-plunger or pushbutton, a burned out transformer, and, of course, loose wires.

Dryers

Most all-electric clothes dryers use 240 volts to power their heating element and usually 120 volts for turning the drum and blowing the air through. Sometimes it can seem as though the heating element must be burned out, while the drum will still turn. This may actually be from one of the dryer's two fuses or half of its double breaker being blown, tripped, or having connection trouble. Don't automatically get a new dryer.

What type of receptacle and cord is appropriate for a dryer? In general, an existing 3-hole dryer receptacle should not be replaced with 4-hole dryer receptacle because there will not usually be a fourth (ground) wire in that box. A 3-prong dryer cord should be installed for an existing 3-hole receptacle, and a 4-prong dryer cord for an existing 4-hole receptacle. In the dryer a metal strap at the neutral (center) terminal should be connected to the frame of the dryer when the cord is 3-prong, and should be disconnected from the frame (or from neutral) for a 4-prong cord, whose green 4th wire connects to the frame.

Generator Switches = Transfer Switches

These panels or switch boxes are meant to make foolproof the powering of home circuits by a generator. Rigging your own way of interfacing the two power sources is liable to be illegal. The switching setup varies with the size of generator and the number and size of circuits to be run by the generator. Some even operate automatically when an outage hits, starting the generator in the process. Power is fed from either the utility or from the generator, through the switch(es) to some individual circuits, a subpanel, or an entire main panel. So even normal power on a fair-weather day has to pass through the switch(es) to reach the chosen circuits. This means that a transfer switch that is turned or knocked off unknowingly will disrupt some power on a day no one is thinking about the generator. Since people are trained to check, at the most, breakers and GFCIs when they lose power somewhere in the house, the generator box can be overlooked.

Two other little problems show up if one of the circuits run by the generator has a GFCI circuit breaker in the main panel and there is a transfer switch for that individual circuit. First, when the circuit is using generator power, it will not be protected from ground-faults, because that GFCI device is now isolated from the circuit. But secondly, when utility power comes on while the generator is still running this circuit, the GFCI breaker in the main panel, being now energized, will be able to sense if some load current is on the neutral wire (which is not isolated) and will notice that none is yet flowing on its hot wire, which is still isolated from the circuit. Since that would constitute an imbalance, the GFCI breaker in the panel would trip., When you transferred everything back to utility power, the circuit in question would be found to be not working and you would have to reset the breaker. But no harm done. All of this would also be true of arc-fault breakers [105], which incorporate ground-fault protection in them.

Hair Dryers

When Code began requiring a dedicated 20-amp circuit for bathroom outlets (1996), U.S. hair dryer manufacturers largely began selling 1800 watt (15-amp) hair dryers almost exclusively. This was fine for homes built since then, but most homes built before that still have 15-amp circuits serving those receptacles, often shared by lights and other outlets in the area. So overloads that trip the circuit breaker are even more common from hair dryer use than used to be the case. Unless you can run yours on a lower-watt setting, the only solution is to have a new dedicated 20-amp circuit run to such receptacles.

Hot Tubs

Water, electricity, and people don't mix well. In the National Electrical Code, hot tubs fall in the same category as swimming pools and are subject to extra safety provisions. One of these requirements (since 1996) is that the electric line feeding most tubs be protected by a ground-fault circuit interrupter. It is commonly a special 120/240 volt circuit breaker that trips off for an electrical leak as small as .005 amps. If this breaker only trips when a certain component of the tub is turning on, it is likely to be that part of the equipment that is faulty. If the breaker has never stayed on from when it was installed, the chances of its being defective are still not as great as its having been hooked up incorrectly, nor as great as the tub's having a basic ground-fault somewhere in its equipment. I have found one or two cases where a tub that had sat idle for a month or two would not let the GFCI breaker turn on. I got a non-GFCI breaker to warm everything up for a day or so and drive moisture or ghosts out of the tub equipment. Then the GFCI breaker, back in place, held.

Light Bulbs

Light fixtures with standard sockets will accept a standard pear-shaped bulb of almost any wattage, but most fixtures are only designed to handle the heat of 60-watt bulbs or less. Anyone unaware of this is likely to replace burned out bulbs with hotter ones, either accidentally or in order to get more light. This will tend to slowly cook the fixture and the nearby ceiling – not a good idea. Running a bulb with too high a wattage can also make a recessed light turn itself off and later back on. This is from a built-in feature meant to prevent exactly the cooking I mention.

The wattage of bulbs also needs to be limited when they are to be controlled by dimmers or motion sensors. Common limits for these are 600 watts and 300 watts respectively (total watts of all bulbs being controlled) . Any dimmer switch will always produce some noticeable heat in itself when operating, but a dimmer [105] running too many watts will be extremely hot.

For some reasons that bulbs burn out prematurely, see [98].

Besides these incandescent bulbs, fluorescent bulbs and tubes are common. Replacing the straight fluorescent tubes can be tricky. If they don't twist into place right, they won't work right. On the other hand, twisting too forcefully can break an end socket. If the fixture has two or more tubes and isn't working very well, it is best to replace them all with brand new ones. From the store is more reliable than from the shelf. The tubes work in pairs, so that if one of two tubes is bad, neither will work well. This is one reason it is simpler to get all new. The other reason is that tubes will tend to die around the same time as each other anyway.

Compact fluorescent bulbs that screw into a standard socket are good energy-savers. However, they have a limitation that is not well known. Most dimmer switches and most electronic timers are not designed to work with these bulbs. These special switches will meet, or dish out, an early death if they try.

Microwave Ovens

Some microwaves on the market use as much as 15 amps when running. So they can easily contribute to a breaker tripping from overload, even in a new kitchen that is supplied with 20-amp outlet circuits. But a very common tripping situation exists, regardless of the microwave's power, wherever it has been mounted over a stove – where an exhaust hood used to be – without providing a stronger circuit for it. The hoods tended to be wired on a general-purpose 15-amp circuit shared with other lights and rooms. Such areas will also often show a noticeable dimming when the microwave runs. The solution to such tripping is to have a new dedicated circuit run for the microwave.

Motion Sensors

Lights that have a motion sensor to switch them typically have the following features. Motion is sensed from the heat emitted by people, animals or cars within the field of view of the device. They also sense light so as to prevent operation during daylight. This feature can be bypassed when using a "test" mode. There are usually settings for how sensitive you want them to be. This is equivalent to the distance away it will sense motion, I believe. There is also a setting for how long they keep the light on after motion is sensed or after motion stops.

So when a problem arises with a motion-activated light, check all these settings and, of course, the light bulbs themselves. One common feature is that a brief interruption of power to the sensor light (and you can do this purposely) may program it to stay on indefinitely or at least till the next dawn. To escape this mode usually involves turning power off for a longer time before restoring power.

Being electronic, and some being cheap, motion sensors die, often within five or ten years. The sensor part might be replaceable, but whole fixtures that incorporate sensors are very common, and many are cheaper than a separate sensor.

Photocells = Photoelectric Switches

Photocells turn lights on at dusk and off at dawn. Some, but not all, are rated to control quite a few lights, including fluorescent. When they fail, the result is commonly that their lights stay on all the time. Of course, if shrubbery has overgrown the area of the photocell or if paint or algae has accumulated on its "window," then the lights could be staying on, or staying on later into the morning, for these reasons.

Range (Plug-In Variety)

See Dryers [105] regarding the right receptacle and cord to use, but use one appropriate to a range, not a dryer. Also, like a dryer, the failure of the oven, or a burner or two, to heat can sometimes be due to half of the 240-volt power being poorly connected at the cord, receptacle, breaker/fuse, panel, or power company.

Receptacles = Outlets

Receptacles do a lot of slave labor for us, so that we take them for granted – until they give us trouble. It helps to distinguish localized trouble from system trouble. If a receptacle, or even a few in different parts of the home, have occasional trouble running things, and this is affected by manipulating the cord-end as it is plugged in or out, the receptacle is probably worn out. By this I mean that the receptacle's springy receivers, which hold on to the prongs of the cord being plugged in, are bent or "sprung" from multiple use or abuse. This is very common at receptacles that are out in the open in a room or hall, that is, where the vacuum cleaner is often used. When the vacuum cord is stretched to its limit, it will be pulling (sideways) on the receivers, bending them. To bend a cord's own prongs to match is a poor stop-gap solution. Such receptacles need replacement.

On the other hand, if the outage is solid, long-lasting, and affects other outlets in the same area, it has something to do with the electrical system. The simplest possibilities include a tripped breaker or ground-fault circuit interrupter (GFCI). Resetting a GFCI involves pushing its reset button in. Finding the right GFCI [31] is another matter. A tripped circuit breaker [62] is reset by first turning it very firmly off, then on. If it wants to retrip quickly, a short circuit [56] is happening. One origin of short circuits has to do with receptacles. If the screw that holds the coverplate to a receptacle is longer than usual, it can break the receptacle apart internally and set up a short.

Beyond these, a system outage will be from a poor connection (an open) somewhere along the circuit. The problem's location will occasionally show itself as a browning or discoloration visible on the face of a receptacle or its cover – signs of heat damage. If not, see [58]. If heat itself is felt at a receptacle, this can also be a sign that a connection is in trouble and about to give up. However, heat and browning will sometimes have to do with a particular heavy load – a space heater, for instance – that has been used at that particular receptacle. That would fall back in the "localized trouble" category. In either case, that receptacle would need to be replaced and its wire connections improved.

Smoke Alarms

A smoke alarm is often "direct wired," whether it has a battery as backup in addition or not. Such a 120-volt alarm will often also be interconnected with others in the home by means of a third insulated wire – usually red in the house-wiring and yellow or orange from the alarm. When there is such interconnection, it can be hard to determine which alarm is setting all of them off. One alarm may not be replaceable except with an alarm of the exact same brand and model. So replacing all at once may be necessary. When alarms include batteries, they may sound a signal of some sort to warn you that the battery is low.

Space Heaters

By design, most homes have permanent heating equipment. However, the use of a portable space heater is common when the main heat source is inadequate or when a particular room or person has a need to supplement or control heat individually. But the capacity of circuits for bedrooms rarely anticipates this. These are commonly 15-amp circuits which may extend to carry the electrical load of two additional rooms. So overloading such a circuit – tripping its breaker – is common when heaters are in use. The fact that many portable heaters now include a switch for choosing a wattage lower than the usual maximum of 1500 watts, doesn't always occur to people. They like the way the full wattage warms a cool room up faster. Besides using the lower-watt setting or getting a heater that has this feature, the solution to these overloads would be to run a dedicated circuit to a new receptacle in each room needing more heat, or to consider running circuits for permanent in-wall or on-wall heaters.

Switched Outlets

By Code most rooms must have a light, which is to be controlled by a wall-switch. Since home designers may want the appearance and placement of lights to be versatile, receptacles for portable lamps in bedrooms, living, family, and other rooms are allowed to be what is switched, rather than permanent fixtures.

In the 1950s and 1960s, an entire outlet or two in these rooms was switched. Since then it has been more common to switch just the top or bottom half of our usual "duplex" receptacles. This has been made possible by the fact that the top and bottom halves of modern receptacles are electrically connected by two accessible and removable metal tabs to the right and left of the center of an upright-mounted receptacle. See examples in the Typical Circuit [21].

For only half of such a receptacle to be switched, the tab on the hot side must be broken off by bending it back and forth several times. The wire that is made hot by the switch is connected at the receptacle to a hot-side terminal on the top (or bottom) half, with wires that are always hot connected on the other half. The neutral (white) wires are all connected anywhere on the "white" side of the receptacle, and the tab on that side should be left in place. Any wire (usually red) that is supposed to go on to another receptacle in the room to switch half of it as well, needs to connect to the hot side on the same half as the one made hot by the switch.

If receptacles have recently been replaced in a room, and the switch for the room no longer turns any receptacle off, then hot-side tabs have probably not been removed from those new receptacles. The presence of a red switching wire attached to a new receptacle will tend to mean it had been switched before. If all the hot-side tabs at all such places in the room are not broken off, the switch will not be able to turn lamps off anymore at *any* of those places.

Thermostats

See [90]. Hooking up a thermostats may present problems. Manufacturers of 240-volt thermostats indicate which of their wires is to attach to the incoming line wire(s) and which to the outgoing load wire(s). I am not aware that the reversing of these makes any difference.

More confusing is the hookup of a 2-pole thermostat, especially where it is replacing a single-pole thermostat (or vice versa). If the one or two cable-pairs of wires that go to the heater(s) are connected to the wires marked "load," and the one or two cable-pairs of wires bringing or sending the constant voltage, are attached to the "line" wires, then things should work. But suppose you are replacing a single-pole thermostat and brought a double-pole home from the store. Yes, you might attach just one side of the double thermostat to the two (black) wires you unhooked the old single from. But it matters which side of the double-pole thermostat you use. This is because most *double-pole thermostats are fake*. By this I mean, one half is a normal single pole thermostat, but the other is only set up as an on/off switch, not heat related. So if you were to hook to the on/off side only, the thermostat would only act like a switch – always on till you clicked it off at the very bottom end of the dial.

Timers

Here I am referring to switches that mount in normal electrical boxes and control what time of day (outdoor) lights will turn on and off. Some are completely mechanical, having a motor that turns a clock past on-off trippers. These are actually the most reliable. Others are electronic and are usually more limited in the total wattage and type of bulb (incandescent) they can control. Some won't even work or give a read-out if the bulbs are all burned out. Electronic timers are shorter-lived, being vulnerable to surges.

Two-Hole Receptacles

Electrical boxes were commonly provided with grounding wires only beginning in the mid-1960s. But over the years, many homes built before then have been given ground-type receptacles (3-holes) in order to physically accommodate 3-prong cords. Unless new cables or ground wires were run to these outlets, however, these receptacles are lying, seeming to promise grounding when there is none. And the simple 3-hole outlet tester used by inspectors [73] at the time a home is being sold will reveal this. Such outlets may revert to having 2-slot receptacles – still available and legal for that situation. Or outlets can be given a ground wire back to the panel from each circuit being grounded. Or the outlets may be protected by a GFCI, though this won't help surge protector strips do their job. See [74].

Water Heaters

Typical household electric water heaters these days run about 4500 watts through one of two elements at a time. Each element has its own thermostat, whose temperature setting can be adjusted. When the upper element, where hot water first leaves the tank, has achieved the temperature it was set for, its thermostat switches the current down to the lower element to prepare more hot water to replace whatever might be drawn off from the upper part of the tank. If both thermostats achieve their setting, no more current flows. Of the two thermostats, the upper one has a reset button that will pop out and keep both thermostats from running current through their elements. This occurs if water there has gotten extremely hot – usually when one of the thermostats is stuck on and needs to be replaced. If the water heater itself is fairly new when this happens, it doesn't make sense to have a plumber replace the whole thing when probably only a thermostat is at fault. On the off-chance that the button's popping off was just a one time thing, simply pushing it back in will restore operation.

X-10 Switching

This high-tech type of switching is used with "smart homes." These systems program lights and appliances to operate as commanded, remotely or according to conditions. If the people who inherit such a system are not as smart as it is, this technology may be not so smart after all. In any case, I have not had much call to troubleshoot these systems, but the manufacturers' and retailers' representatives have. If you think you have such a system, check the internet for help.

CHAPTER 22

Brief Troubleshooting Tips

Is electrical troubleshooting for a home simple? Sometimes Yes. Sometimes No. If you read this guide thoroughly, you will realize that more is involved than other resources suggest. You may wonder if it is more than you want to deal with. But with increased understanding you are more equipped to address your particular problem.

The bulk of home electrical wiring problems can be divided into three classes. Outright mistakes in installation or connection. Inferior connecting. The shortcomings of materials.

The voltage in half of all U.S. and Canadian homes is greater than most light bulbs are designed to run on.

There are three things people imagine, which I have come across only once at the most. A breaker that trips only from mechanical weakness. A person who can testify that they were being shocked and then a GFCI tripped and saved them. Signs that a rodent has chewed on housewire simply for fun. (I did hear that rodents which have been poisoned will chew on things randomly.)

A circuit breaker can appear to be on, but really be tripped.

Should you be afraid of overloading your circuits? Generally not, because you have circuit breakers! They stop overloads in their tracks by tripping the circuit off before a load gets "over." Still, you might say, we can't tell when some trusted electrical component might be faulty and overheat. True, but that is an unexpected "undercapacity," not an overloading on your part. The main exception to this is the overloading of light fixtures or extension cords, not whole circuits. These state the maximum wattages they are to serve and do not usually have built-in trip-offs. So pay attention with those. But don't worry about using your circuits. Life is too short.

The resistance of an incandescent light bulb filament is very much less when measured with power off than when carrying its current.

In some cases a circuit breaker will trip off only after the circuit has been running things for 15 minutes or more. This might not be from an overload but from a poor connection point at, or in, the breaker itself, which develops heat that fools the breaker.

When part of a circuit goes dead due to an open neutral, people testing their wires are surprised to find white wires registering hot (live). An outlet tester calls the condition "hot and ground reversed," but what is really happening is this. Somewhere among the non-working items, a turned-on one lets hotness through its resistance but since it no longer has a path or connection back to the panel (the usual neutral), those whites still show hotness. They are able to shock you in fact!

A normal receptacle is sometimes ground-fault protected from elsewhere.

Certainly, many electrical problems come from homeowners "doing-it-themselves." Many also come from poor work by professionals. (Or is that a contradiction in terms?) But when the populace is kept ignorant and kept away from practical knowledge of their own property, this can be expected. If doing-it-yourself were encouraged more, I think the level of competence in the whole community would increase.

Home electricity doesn't flow in one constant direction.

Three assumptions that can be wrong: The breaker is responsible for things on a circuit being dead. The loose connection along a circuit will be found at one of the circuit's dead items. You can't get shocked at an outlet that doesn't work.

A turned-on dimmer switch normally produces some heat.

Most of a circuit can stop working even when the breaker is on and is fine.

A GFCI receptacle will not trip for an overload.

When on their high setting, hair dryers sold today will use the entire capacity of a 15-amp circuit.

A breaker trips much more often for a real short or overload than from some defect in itself.

A GFCI almost never trips from a defect in it. Usually a GFCI trips from being miswired, or from a fault in something that is plugged into it or into a regular outlet protected by it.

If you lose power to much of a circuit, the first of the dead things may have the poor connection, but it is equally likely that the last of the working things has a wire poorly connected from it.

GFCI outlets nowadays won't allow you to reset them if the power to them is off.

Upgrading an electrical panel to greater space or current-capacity does nothing (by itself) to alleviate the overloading of a particular circuit. It may even make overloads more frequent, if someone in the past had increased the amperage of a fuse or breaker.

What are people's three worst fears about their home wiring? First, that something will go wrong with the wires back in the wall, where it's hard to know about or do something about. Second, that it will have been caused by a malicious chewing varmint. And third, that this is sure to start a fire. Each of these scenarios by itself is rare. Imagine how rare they are together. Most problems live safely and conveniently within the electrical boxes that are required.

CHAPTER 23

Some Thoughts on "Electrical" Fires

Regarding electrical safety, there is certainly some need to warn the innocent, the ignorant, and the foolhardy about hazards involved with electrical installation, repair, and investigation. However, I do think there are two unfortunate results of the excessive, repetitive warnings encouraged by the safety industry and our suing society. One is that the public is led away from common sense and a desire to understand electrical things, away from normal confidence, into a general paranoia. The other result can be a disdain for any printed cautions because they are seen to be merely generic and needed to satisfy lawyers and insurance companies, and because they can in fact usually be ignored without harm.

Experience tells many of us that warning statements containing the verb, "may," can be translated just as well by "very rarely." Indeed using a product improperly may cause serious injury or death. On the other hand, we can get away with a lot of supposed misuse without a problem, and it is sometimes convenient to do so in spite of risks.

My main safety warning to those involved in troubleshooting is found at [5]. If you should happen to get shocked in spite of your best informed efforts, hopefully it will be a wake-up call to learn from. The fact that I have been mildly shocked a number of times has made me more aware of what I am doing, and a better electrician. I have not gotten used to being shocked, but I honestly must tell you that most shocks are mild and not life-threatening.

Besides shocks, the other usual electrical warning is aimed at fire hazard. It is true that electrical practices mandated by the National Electrical Code are especially designed to reduce the risk of fire from electrical installations. I am of the opinion that the likelihood of building combustion directly due to poorly done electrical systems is portrayed as much higher than statistics would reveal, if exact statistics on this were abundant, available, and interpreted carefully. See "What Is An Electrical Fire?" [116]. When there is no other obvious cause, fire investigators do often call it electrical, when there is no such positive evidence. It would in fact be difficult to purposely start a fire by intentionally shoddy electrical work.

During a given year in my area of the U.S., I see about one hundred instances of the most common form of wires overheating at connection points. I can safely say that, combined with the other contractors in the same area, we see at least 5000 of these. Some of them are quite ugly-looking [119], and a few of these might have been capable of starting a fire if other conditions had been favorable. But other conditions were not favorable; that's why we were able to come to the home – it was still standing. True, we don't get called to the ones that do start fires. But I believe those amount to less than five instances per year in the same geographic area, and perhaps as little as one. So, I contend that a small fraction of one percent of these bad connections will start fires. Apparently that is enough for the safety industry to justify any product or regulation that is believed to reduce the statistic.

I believe that the Code and its enforcement are largely justifiable for reasons other than fire hazard alone. Operational reliability, shock hazard, and uniformity of practice are rather important. Most electrical conditions that do happen to result in fires would already have violated one of these values. Troubleshooting itself would be much more complicated if there were no established standards of installation. Ignorant homeowners who violate the Code risk not only a measure of fire hazard, but a likelihood of electrical interruptions and sub-par performance – tripping from overloads, deterioration of components, reduced voltage, flickering of lights, etc. These things do not get the monetary attention of the insurance and safety industries, but they deserve prohibition simply in the name of consumer protection.

What Is An Electrical Fire?

This heading gives my views on a subject that has not had sufficient research to support or refute my views. I trust you will take them for what they are.

The public has not been encouraged to distinguish fire danger arising from electrically powered things (or their abuse) from fire danger arising out of imperfections in an electrical system (due to design or installation). Fires from this second matter certainly deserve the name "electrical." It must still be understood that any fire that is destructive beyond the malfunctioning electrical system equipment itself (destructive, that is, of people or belongings) is actually a structural fire, and depends on the proximity of combustibles to such electrical equipment.

By this definition, for example, fires originating from light fixtures that overheat from bulbs of excessive wattage are not electrical. Nor is a fire from bedding blocking the airflow of an electric heater, unless the heater's safety device failed to shut it down. Also an arcing short from someone's having nailed a cord along the surface of a wall would not be an "electrical" fire as I am defining it. It would be a case of abuse of an electrical consumable, not a case of improper installation of the electrical distribution system.

It could be that over an indefinitely long time, every electrical component installed in every home could deteriorate to the point of presenting a slight fire hazard. The design, approval, and installation of these components does not take into consideration such a long period of time, during which many kinds of conditions can have an effect on their integrity. Nor could there be an economical way of requiring such longevity from the beginning. We assume the need for some maintenance and for eventual replacement – even of the building itself. Whether the maintenance done is preventive or is in response to active problems encountered might make some difference in fire statistics, but this has not been shown, that I am aware of. Over-maintenance is possible. Also, since any change made can awaken existing imperfections or contain imperfections of its own, total safety will never be a realistic goal.

Of all home fires 1994-1998, about 3%* were due to electrical system failures, as I have defined them, compared with 2% from natural causes. I sympathize with some of the distrust the public has developed for electrical things in general, but not all of it, because this has been an area of considerable hype.

*The U.S. Fire Administration categorized 9.4% as "electrical distribution" fires. Within this category, however, is included lamps, light fixtures, and lamp and extension cords, which are certainly electrical but by their portable nature or product nature should not so easily be lumped with what the electrical trade is responsible for. My alternate figure of 3% comes from breaking down the causes of 149 of these "electrical and lamp" fires found in the study *Residential Electrical Distribution Fires* by the U.S. Consumer Product Safety Commission (1987). The subcategories in that report could not always distinguish between mechanical damage and poor installation, and do not reveal enough to mount a campaign against all the true causes. For instance, overheating at a receptacle may be from the looseness of the wires attached by the electrician to it or from looseness of its slots that receive what you plug into it. After a fire it is not easy to tell the difference. Looseness in the slots is common and is a case of mechanical damage, often from plugged-in cords being pulled sideways – as when going too far away with a vacuum.

Signs of Heat From Loose Electrical Connections

The items in the photo (opposite) had reached a point that they stopped the operation of part of their circuit. The appearance of these is extreme. For how to recognize the more usual cases, see [77]. Some types of the poor connections are shown in [17].

A. The "hot" side of these two receptacles did get hot. Both were using screw terminals to hold their aluminum wires. The plastic of the one on the left suffered so much that the screws and metal plug-receivers that are usually held captive pulled right out. The one on the right was fairly new, replacing an older receptacle. But since the wires were aluminum, which doesn't get along well with the alloys of most receptacles, these connections didn't last long. Only receptacles that say COALR are to connect aluminum wires directly to their terminals.

B. These two also had trouble on the "hot" side, but now it is copper wire. What caused the connections to go bad? Perhaps the person installing did not seat the loop of copper evenly and directly under the screw, did not tighten the screw enough, or curled the copper counterclockwise under the screw (so that tightening actually squeezed the loop apart and outward). Or maybe they were not careful to insure that only metal ended up trapped under the screw; see [41].

C. Likewise, here are two hot wires that led dysfunctional lives.

D. This wires-in-hole style receptacle is shown from its back side. The darkness around the push-in holes tells us that heat had developed at both hot and neutral wire connection points.

E. This is the socket of a common porch light. The heat it suffered was from running 75- or 100-watt bulbs in a fixture designed to dissipate only the heat of a 60-watt bulb.

F. This underground cable was shorting in the earth, begun by a shovel's nick. I find that an underground cable doesn't short into the actual earth significantly. It is enabled to short from its exposed hot over to its own ground wire, by the conductivity of the moisture and soil that is right along the surface of the cable.

G. These two aluminum-wired receptacles suffered their heat on the neutral side. The insulation on the wires of the left hand receptacle melted and vaporized back about two inches from the source of the heat (at the screws). In my experience, three inches is as far as I see things go, whether for aluminum or copper wire. By that time the connection has gotten so poor it doesn't let current flow through it anymore. So the heating process is self-defeating – usually. Under some conditions, the heat does reach and ignite combustible materials.

H. Here copper had a poor connection on the neutral side.

I. These are the ends of three neutral wires. They may have been attached to receptacles, or their poor contact may have been in wire connectors.

J. The discoloration of this receptacle at one of its slots is typical of poor pressure of the receptacle's receivers on the cord-prongs plugged into them. Receivers get sprung apart this way by repeated plugging in and out, and when a cord is pulled sideways.

K. This is a clothes dryer cord-plug (on the left) and what is left of one receiver (on the right) of that dryer's receptacle. The source of the heat was the receiver being sprung apart too far. This is the same situation as in "J," but on a 240-volt 30-amp scale.

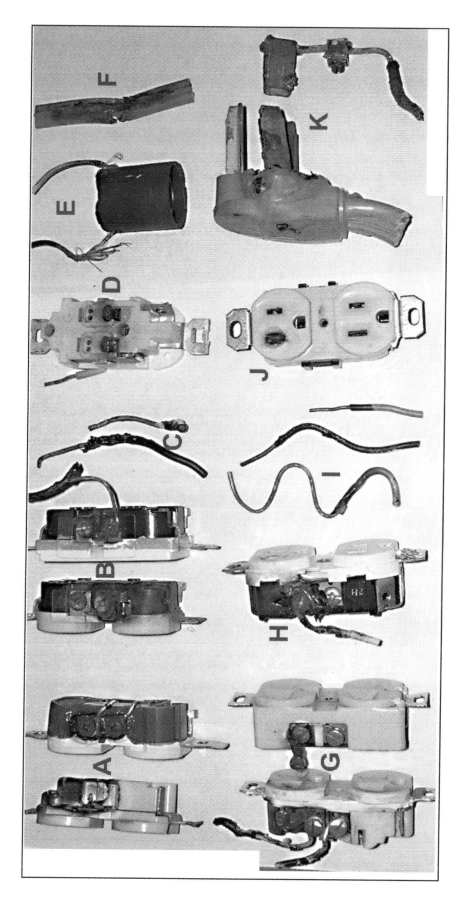

CHAPTER 24

Stories: Detective Cases

These true stories from my past might be of interest. Enjoy them even when you don't quite understand them. I didn't understand them either, till I got to the Aha! Moment.

The Solid Brass Chandelier

I learned something new about vintage light fixtures when I was called to an old mansion. The woman reported that one particular circuit was tripped and wouldn't go back on. Sure enough, a short of some kind.

Now, many people apologize to me for the mess their house is in, thinking that I care. If anything, clutter adds to the challenge, although I do prefer electrical challenges. This woman was apologizing too. She had a lot of stuff around. But as I was getting acquainted with the problem circuit, I saw a closed door that she seemed to be shying me away from. "What's in there," I said. "Oh, you don't want to go in there," she said. I managed to convince her that I needed to and that I didn't care what it looked like. In I went.

I truly don't remember it being that bad. What I did notice, however, was that, like the other bedrooms I had looked at, this one had a heavy and ornate old chandelier. On the "arms" of this one, though, she had hung a lot of clothes, using wire-type hangers. Ordinarily that would not be noteworthy, but these fixtures had the two wires for each bulb running along the top of each arm, not inside the arms (solid brass, not hollow). As I looked closely, I did see that one of these fixture wires was worn bare against the metal because of a hanger. But this house is so old, I thought, the metal won't be grounded, so how could a short occur? My answer was on another arm of the chandelier, where another wire (of the opposite polarity, I gathered) was also held bare against the metal. So this was a hot-to-neutral short through the metal of the fixture. I don't remember how I repaired this, but I had a little talk with my customer about where she was going to hang her clothes from now on.

How Animals Like Electricity

Two or three times I have found receptacles with very corroded parts and connections. And the homeowners did not hesitate to blame it on their poor cat. They had either seen or suspected that the cat had marked and remarked territory by aiming at receptacles – indoors! The cats that lived to remark, I mean.

Another critter whose chemistry does a number on copper is ants; like when they hole up for the winter in your outlet box. I've seen a pile of ladybugs in a warm panel. And there have been mice turned into dry statues in a panel, when stepping innocently from one main wire to the other. And once, a garden grub had gotten into an outdoor receptacle, who was conductive enough, even in death, to make the breaker trip till I located and removed him.

On a positive note, animals can be a troubleshooter's best friend. A little dog once tipped me off to the short circuit location by his sniffing there. Wish I had a dog like that. When looking for a short buried in the ground, I have occasionally set voltage going that got worms to come to the surface right in the area of a short!

Invigorating Shower

This woman was shocked during a shower and on another day shocked so badly in the tub, she went to the hospital with possible heart damage. I found the hot and cold water lines were well grounded, but the metal waste/drain/vent pipes were not necessarily. In the attic I saw that one of these BX (spiral armored) cables came up from an outlet in the room bordering this bathroom and was spliced to older knob and tube wires; but before it reached the knob and tube wires, it was lying against the plumbing vent pipe coming up from the tub drain area.

Well, she admitted that she had wanted the 2-hole receptacle in that room changed to a 3-hole grounded receptacle, so she had had a friend work on it. What I found he had done was this. The BX's wires had a braided look, and the black was not easily distinguishable from the white. He had taken what he thought was the white and connected it not only to the white side of the receptacle but also to the receptacle's ground screw, which would have grounded it illegally. One reason that is not the way to get a ground is this very mix-up he made – he had used the hot wire thinking it was the neutral.

The effect of this was that the metal yoke of the receptacle, being one with the ground screw, was now passing hotness on to the metal box, and the box passed it on to the cable's armor, and the armor passed it on to the vent pipe, which was one with the tub's drain pipe, which passed it on through *her*, up through the showering water to the grounded water pipes. I made the outlet back into the 2-hole type and grounded the waste/vent pipes for the first time.

Not All There

A few things were dead after Dave says he was cutting a lamp-cord shorter. With it still plugged in. Yes, live! He admitted to being not all there. Now this lamp was plugged in near a GFCI in the kitchen. Trying to reset the GFCI made no difference. After all, the cord he cut was just two-wire. That wouldn't bother a GFCI anyway. But it should have bothered the breaker. Show me the panel! Again things looked OK on first glance. But that double-pole 20-amp felt a little different. Why a double pole for two circuits? There can be reasons. Anyway, I reset it.

Troubleshooting With Prayer

Jim's well circuit would not stay on. There was a short-circuit somewhere along its 700-foot line. My tester showed the path the line took in the ground, but was not as helpful pinpointing the bad spot. It didn't help that the buried wires were two paralleled 10-2s, spliced every 250 feet or so. I bit the bullet and dug down at three places, each time cutting the line, measuring its resistance, and putting it back together. A bit of praying allowed me to find the exact spot to repair at my fourth hole! (When wires of an underground cable are not separated from each other enough, the grounds may be close enough to a semi-poor splice of hots to short to it.) The process was time-consuming but much less costly than someone digging a whole new line in. I hope I haven't made this one sound easy. It wasn't.

Personal Experience Helps

Dave had told me that lights would dim down at times in various rooms. I wasn't sure he had anything wrong, since this can be normal to a degree when heavy appliances turn on. But I came to check it out. And I did start to observe the voltage dragging down at times. At his main panel I found that some other circuits were being subjected to a little higher than normal voltage. This is typical of a poor main neutral wire.

When I saw the meter equipment outdoors, it was *deja vu*. Dave had the same meter-can brand (early '80s G.E.) that I do at home. I had been through a similar experience of lights dimming rather pronouncedly, until I saw behind my own meter that the power company's main neutral was too small for the clamp-connector in the meter equipment. Just enough that things would run OK but give lights an annoying deep blink. This situation is not healthy for electronics in a home. I went to bat for Dave by calling the power company myself. Will they believe a non-electrician? They promised to come correct the matter.

Toasted Twice

Next a sad story. This man's mobile home had oodles of electronic stuff. Most of it got fried four months ago, he said. The power company thought they found a bad neutral in the transformer and replaced the transformer. Now his next set of stuff fried, some in spite of good surge protectors. Sustained higher voltage isn't like a brief surge. Lights were getting bright, then dim, some of them popping. He was there.

These things weren't happening when I arrived. OK, sounds like the power company was wrong. But we have to be sure the bad main neutral isn't in my customer's meterbox or panel. The panel had no 120-volt circuits sharing a neutral, and the damage wasn't limited to two circuits anyway. The panel neutral was tight and looked good. There is a rigid strap that connects the neutral bar on one side to the other. I thought I saw a little discoloration near one screw holding it together. Nope, it was tight and OK underneath. How about a big junction box underneath the home for the main feed to the panel? Some mobiles have this. I crawled under enough to see there was none.

Then what about the outdoor meter/disconnect on his pole? Neutrals in and out of there checked out. There was even a feed from there directly to his shop building. Did anything out there get hurt? He said it did in June but he hadn't checked this time. We went out there. Garage door opener was dead. Hmmm. This confirmed that the problem was back ahead of the meter setup. I called the power company. But I knew they might not take this comes-and-goes problem seriously enough. And the guy needed to be able to use his computer (it escaped) without anxiety. So I proposed putting all his 120-volt breakers onto the same phase in the panel. That's what I did. That would keep a bad main neutral from getting at them from the other phase [38].

Right as I finished that, the power company showed up. This lineman is used to false alarms. He considers everything I have to say. And the fact that the neighbor off the same transformer had no problem in June or now. He subjects his line to a load test and finds no problem. But, he admits, since I'm still there waiting to see what he'll do, he'll keep looking. He redoes connections atop the meter pole. I'm still there. So he goes up near the transformer. I have to get on to the next job, so I leave. That night my customer calls. He says they found a neutral near the transformer, wiggling in its crimp connector. Wrong size maybe. They gave him the old connector. He'll see if his insurance or the power company will still refuse to reimburse him with that to wave in their faces.

Up On a Mountain

This vacated rental house had an airplane's view. Kitchen lights were dead. No life at the switch. The landlady had her handyman show me where the panel was. Two breakers sat tripped. That was easy. Must have been a little more was dead than she knew.

Then she wanted me to hook up a cooktop that had replaced the old one. I expected a small can of worms. I got a big one. The hookup was actually easy. But why was the line dead when all the breakers were on? She said the old one may not have worked for a while either. Back at the panel I looked for a cooktop-sized cable and found one. It wasn't in the panel. It had been pulled out and replaced by some other cable, which I found went to an illegal generator interface. I pulled it out of the panel and put our cooktop one back in. Some tenant who eats out must have disliked mountain power irregularities.

But the story goes on. Putting our cable back in, I found water sitting on and around the main breaker. Not healthy. Sopped that up fine, but the ugly thing I found was all the neutrals on one side of the panel were toasted. It was the side used by whoever wired the newer parts of the house. They had a light touch with the screwdriver. She said the house would be torn down in a year or two anyway. I said the circuits wouldn't last that long with a tenant using things. So she had me do what I had to do to restore solid connections.

Double Trouble

Outlets and lights dead in parts of a living room, bathroom and a bedroom. In the living room they read "open neutral." In the bath/bedroom just "dead." Hmmm. It did turn out to be two problems on the same circuit. I found the bad neutral in the living room. A melted wirenut, from aluminum wire.

Fine, but now the bath/bed area is still dead. Is it on the same circuit? Only my wire tracer knew for sure. Running signal back on the now-good neutral showed it was the same circuit path as the living room. Where, oh where, is the hot wire bad? Well, after checking at a couple of the first dead things, I went in the attic. The line there was dead from the living room outlet where I had just fixed the neutral! Opened that back up. The black wires weren't melty but they weren't connected well. Now they are.

Persistence and the Power Company

A dimming and/or brightening of lights was happening at David's house at unpredictable times. But I wasn't far away, so I came one evening when it was happening. It was a voltage problem, so we had the power company come check things. Nothing. But since the problem recurred a little later, we had them put a recording-volt-meter on their lines for three days. Nothing! Since it acted up after the three days, I went to bat for Dave. I called up the power company and assured them the trouble wasn't in the house. I told them to try actually redoing two of their main neutral line connections. After they did that, there was no more problem.

The Trouble With Taking a Light Down

Some of Alan's living room plugs and garage lights weren't working. A simple test of that circuit showed me that somewhere along the line one of the neutral wires was broken or loose – but where? After undoing two or three devices to check their connections, I followed a suspicion to the dining room light, which itself was working! Up in its electrical box was the loose junction, probably put together poorly by whoever had taken the light down during recent remodeling.

Lightning and Gas

Ever wonder why Code is so picky about grounding? As a brand-new journeyman I saw an example. My boss sent me to a house where lightning had started a fire somehow. A gas explosion got it going. Gas company found a hole the lightning had blown in their buried pipe. In making a repair to conduit at the same place, I came to realize what had happened.

The gas pipe and the grounded conduit had been touching in the earth. It was easy for the lightning to use that point of contact to try to find a way to ground, but since it wasn't tight contact over a good surface area, it blew a hole. That had let gas leak over into the conduit and into a basement utility room the conduit came from. In that room was an electric water heater, whose thermostat made a spark once it had heated its water. There's your explosion.

Why doesn't this sort of thing happen more often? Because normally the gas pipe would have been "bonded" (made electrically solid) to the conduit by a wire and pipe clamps. This should have been done out in the swimming pool pump house to which the gas and conduit were running. Out there I looked for this bond and found the bond wire and one clamp, but for lack of a second clamp on the truck (apparently) the bonding had never been completed. Little things can matter.

High price

Bob had been given a high price by an electrician, to change the main breaker in his panel. A second opinion from me was that the main breaker was fine, but two smaller breakers were making poor contact in the panel. I found better places for them in the panel. Bob had been about to buy a new dryer because it didn't put out any heat even after he gave it a new element. I saved him that expense too: the dryer breaker was one of the ones that had been doing poorly till I moved it. He can do laundry now.

Fridge Shock

Hester was getting shocked when she touched her fridge and the stove at the same time or the fridge and the sink. The common denominator is the fridge, I figured, but is that my problem or one for the appliance guy? My testers confirmed that the frame of the fridge was energized. I took a quick peek underneath it – nothing obvious. This was an older fridge without a third prong (ground wire) on its cord. I wondered why she hadn't been shocked before. Finally I plugged it in the right way (turned the cord end over), and the stray voltage was gone. There is a neutral wire touching metal somewhere inside her fridge, but there is no more danger unless someone reverses the cord end again. Call the appliance repair people.

Factory Cover-up

Here's a good one. A breaker in Pat's garage tripped and wouldn't reset. Fortunately all the wiring was still accessible (no sheetrock). I traced the short to a place along one cable. I opened the cable and found that the factory had made a black wire splice inside it but hadn't taped or insulated it. This is very rare. The splice had finally come close enough to the bare ground wire next to it to short over. I repaired it with a junction box.

Faulty

Don was right to suspect that the GFCI was tripping off for something outdoors. After all, his fountain was on that line, and we know that water and electricity don't mix without potential problems. An outlet or two in the living room were on the line affected by the GFCI, and the GFCI itself, of course, which was in the garage. But as I got acquainted with the circuit, I discovered that an old refrigerator, also in the garage, was actually responsible. With it unplugged, the fault was gone. If it was worth it to Don, he could have that fridge repaired.

Buried

John has one of the newer homes up on the hill. From the beginning, an outlet in the kitchen and one in the dining room never worked. I poked around for a tripped GFCI or a loose connection on two nearby circuits. But when I checked to see if any of the three wires of the bad cable had continuity to elsewhere, only the bare ground was good. A wire tracer I have pointed me along the wall from the kitchen outlet. This wall should have had two outlets by Code, but only had the one. More often than you would think, drywallers cover electrical boxes. Usually I can narrow down where to cut in for the box by holding a straight-edge against the wall till I notice a bulge. No bulge this time. Some other tests made me brave, and sure enough I found the box and gave it a receptacle so that the dead ones could come to life.

Dinner Party Pressure

Downstairs was this mother-in-law apartment. Its dining room outlets and light were not working and she was to entertain guests there that evening. I had to pull out all my tricks for this one, and it took me a few hours. I knew there was a bad connection along the circuit, but when I had checked at all the obvious visible outlet boxes, I began to wonder if this was one of those rare splices in the wall – no box.

My wire tracer showed me where the bad wire went in the walls till it was bad. The suspect place was in a wall behind kitchen cabinets or (other side of same wall) behind a bathroom cabinet. I pulled drawers out. In the bathroom I opened an exploratory hole and felt a wire and a box in the wall. Since it seemed to be facing the other way, toward kitchen, I measured and opened another hole behind the drawers of a kitchen cabinet. There was a receptacle that had been left buried behind these cabinets when the kitchen was remodeled four years before. And this outlet was having a problem with one of its connections that was supposed to pass the circuit along. I made the repair and turned that box into a junction box with a blank cover.

I think the mother-in-law was happy. The whole time, she and I had been in each other's way in the kitchen, because, for her part, she was very busy cooking up some special things for that dinner.

Apprentice Shortage

Michael was preparing for a generator transfer setup by identifying his circuits. Anything would be an improvement over the scant, generic labeling his panel had come with. In the process he found that to turn off a certain set of lights and outlets, he had to turn off two different circuit breakers. If either breaker was on (with the other off) everything still worked. This could be dangerous for anyone working on either circuit. There were meant to be two circuits leaving the panel. They had been joined to each other somewhere out in the house. But where?

A job for the detective. I had just come from a job the day before where I found a similar mixing of circuits at a double-box, a place they have a chance to mix. So I poked my nose into two or three such candidates without any luck. But a fact was nagging at me – these two circuits left the panel in the same cable with each other, sharing one neutral. Normally, to do that, they would have been given breakers that were 240 volts apart, so as not to overload that neutral. I looked into outlet boxes where this two-circuit cable could be expected to land, but did not see any telltale red wire of the second circuit.

Finally I wondered if an outlet had been covered up (like in the story above) by this big bookcase in the family room. No, Michael said, not covered, just behind the books! That was a relief. I promptly found the outlet, opened it up, saw the red wire, and saw that someone (an apprentice?) had connected things there as if he was dealing with a normal single circuit. That must have set up a 240-volt short, which he, or his journeyman, solved (improperly) by moving one of the breakers to the same "phase" as the other (zero volts apart). I separated these at this outlet and rearranged them at the panel. Now the breakers could once again live 240 volts apart, which their neutral appreciates.

Don't Side With an Electrician

No one likes the thought of a short circuit happening in the wall, where you can't see it or get to it. This problem was close to that. The man of the house had already looked in some electrical boxes of the circuit. But then he told me that one time the breaker didn't trip till his wife turned on the front lights. By undoing certain wires at these lights, I narrowed the short down to the light by the front door *or* the wire in the wall from the switch inside, out to this light. Actually, the wires behind the light came directly out of the siding, but I knew from the missing ground wire that there was probably a box behind the siding.

I'm not a carpenter, but I pulled two boards off as carefully as I could. There was a metal box! And there were a few suspicious long sheathing nails near the path the cable was taking in the wall. It turned out after exonerating the nails, that the short was not in the wall but at the light's box. The electrician who had run the cable into that box had tightened the clamp to hold the cable so tightly it began to short, these several years later. I was able to repair the wire and get the siding back on pretty well, for an electrician.

It Isn't Brain Surgery

My wife and I remember the daughter of an old high school friend of ours. When paying us a visit and hearing what I do, the mother virtually set me up to go to her daughter's place because she knew there was an electrical issue with something there. This girl is now a surgeon. She had taken on some upgrading of switches at home, but things weren't working quite right. I admire the attempt. I'm not equally up to using a scalpel. Anyway, I found the misconnection at a four-way switch for the stairway and showed her how to avoid similar mix-ups elsewhere in the house. I think she'll finish that house-surgery with a healthy patient.

Down Under

When you are new to a house, or when you are selling, are common times for circuit problems to need solving. This man called me because he was alerted to the fact that some of his new home's outlets did not have a good ground reaching them. Usually people aren't aware of this condition because it does not affect normal operation. But he knew he wanted definitely good grounding so that his surge protectors would be capable of protecting his electronic appliances. This home was not an old one that was built before grounds were being wired into buildings. Most of his outlets did show a good ground, and the outlets he was concerned about even showed the bare ground wires in their boxes, hooked up to the receptacles. Where was the continuity of the ground broken?

After looking into the boxes of nearby outlets, I got into my overalls. Why? This was a mobile home, which also has circuit connections underneath it at a "crossover" junction box. By process of elimination, that was almost the only possibility left. Once I found and opened that box, I saw that whoever had joined the wires there when the mobile home was set in place here, had neglected to join the ground wires. Did they have one too few wirenuts? Anyway, I did what he hadn't. It was safe to run the electronics now.

Ground-fault, Short, Overload, or Heat?

I had been to this house before. It has been worked over with remodels and is in heavy use, as a house should be. And the circuit having trouble this time was the same one I had solved a short on before. She described now how the breaker would trip at times that did not correspond exactly to heavy loads. This is a GFCI-type breaker, so there was a question as to whether it was responding to something outdoors in the rain, where the circuit did extend to.

After awhile I took the panel's cover off to check there. There sat the circuit's wire in the breaker with its insulation melted back about two inches. When heat builds up like this from a not-very-tight connection, damage also occurs to the screw-area of the breaker. So I ran after the right breaker at the hardware store, put it in, repaired the wire, and reattached. Case solved.

What had happened was not only a slightly loose wire, but that the heavy loads to this 20-amp breaker were only using 15-amp wire. So some of the overheating was from that. My new breaker was 15-amp rated. I imagine that sometime in the past an original 15-amp breaker had been replaced with the 20 to handle overloads that had been tripping it. I explained all this to the homeowner, and I think she actually understood it. Or maybe she was a good actress.

Endangered Salmon

A recent kitchen remodel at Jim's place seemed fine for awhile. But then a GFCI receptacle there would occasionally trip power off to his refrigerator. Because this was not frequent, it is hard to diagnose. I knew that having a fridge wired downstream from a GFCI is not normal, though it is allowed. It must have been set up that way during the remodel. But now, what if the GFCI trips while Jim is away for a week? Goodbye frozen salmon. So I was at least able to connect things differently at the GFCI receptacle, so that the fridge would no longer be subject to it. It could even be that something about the fridge was causing the tripping. It won't now. The circuit breaker will probably handle any important fault.

Confident People

Jonathan had been too confident in his electrical abilities. He was replacing all his switches and receptacles. After he was all done and put power back on, one switch turned everything in the next room off. Another couldn't turn its light off. And some other rooms were just dead. He wasn't distressed; calling me in was just part of the process. I did find and correct seven places he had hooked wires up wrong. Once I had seen how he dealt with the hookups at one or two, I found the rest without too much fuss. He was consistent. And he wasn't embarrassed. Some people get very embarrassed. I guess I don't care if a customer is embarrassed or not. A customer is a customer.

Keeping Lit Like the Joneses

Richard's GFCI was tripping. Something was going on out there on his underground lines to the postlights out front. Normally the thrill of the chase would have me tracing those lines with a tester and maybe digging a hole or two in the ground. In this case though, I said to myself, why is this line being GFCI protected? If there were any receptacles out there in the yard on this line, Code would call for the shock protection. But not if it is buried well and is only for lights, and it was. I still considered whether the tripping was an indication of a full-blown short happening in the future. That bridge could be crossed later. I gave the line straight power. It didn't short. Richard had his lights back. In some of these neighborhoods, it is part of the covenant to keep your postlights running. I explained to him that the GFCI could have been responding to something of no importance, but to let me know if anything funny developed. He was good with that.

CHAPTER 25

Glossary
Home Electrical Concepts and Components

I think I am using electrical terms in this guide as they are generally used by both electricians and homeowners. Still, there is quite a variety in the terms people are familiar with. If nothing else, the following definitions will let you see what *I* mean by them. Here then is a glossary of electrical terms related to troubleshooting.

Appliance. A non-lighting item that, by its resistance, consumes electricity rather than just passing it on. So an appliance is not a fixture (for lighting) nor a device (for passing on). Examples: fax machine, garbage disposal, even a wired-in smoke alarm perhaps.

Arcing. Current passing across a gap, that is, using the air itself like a short piece of wire.

Arc-fault circuit interrupter = AFCI. A circuit breaker that can also trip for line-to-neutral arcing, that is, arcing short circuits, which might not trip a standard breaker. Required for new bedroom circuits since 2002. Beginning in 2008, they will also trip for series arcing (at poor connections) and will be available in the form of a special receptacle.

Breaker = circuit breaker. A switching device that automatically disconnects power to a circuit when current or heat exceeds a certain level for a certain amount of time. It clips on to one or two hot bus bars in a panel box and passes this hotness through itself to the circuit wire attached to it, normally by means of a screw. Its handle is generally in one of three positions: on, tripped, or off.

Bus bar. A piece of rigid metal within a panel or fuse box which distributes electricity to the various circuits by means of their breakers' connections to it.

Cable. Compare "Wire." A cable is a set of wires, usually encased in an outer protective sheath. A cord would be a cable by this definition so far, but a cable is part of a permanent installation; a cord is more flexible and often has a plug end for a portable appliance or lamp.

Circuit. The actual or intended path of current between points of differing voltage. In the case of a household 120-volt circuit, the path is: along a hot wire at the breaker, through lights/appliances, and along a neutral wire connected to the neutral bar in the panel. In a sense, each loop that current makes (through a single light, for instance) is a circuit, but the most common meaning is the "branch circuit," defined as everything fed (or interrupted) by a given breaker or fuse.

Common. The terminal or wire of a three-way switch which contacts either one or the other of the traveler terminals, depending on the position of the switch.

Current. The flow of electrons in a circuit. This is measured in amps (amperes). In describing 120-volt-driven current we tend to say that it goes "from" a breaker through a light "to" neutral. This directional talk can be misleading, since the actual electrons are moving back and forth sixty times per second. But this way of speaking is similar to how I may say that a highway goes "from" my hometown to the next town, even though the highway simply goes between them and doesn't really start at one or the other.

Device. Distinct from a fixture or appliance, this is an item which does not itself make use of electricity, but interrupts or passes it on in a particular fashion. For example, a switch, a receptacle, a thermostat, a breaker, a fuse.

Dimmer. Also "rheostat." A switch able to dim its lights by altering the voltage it passes on. A dimmer normally gets warm when operating but will overheat if running more wattage than it is designed for.

Electricity. That is, "tame" electricity, not static electricity or lightning. A force generated onto loops of conductive material, transferred through their electrons, and applied as useful energy at parts of these loops.

Fixture. Or "luminaire." A light. Specifically, a non-portable electrically-produced-light assembly. Distinguished from appliance, device, and lamp.

Fuse. A device that interrupts current to its circuit by melting apart. It must then be replaced.

Fuse box. Like a panel, a usual main source of the circuits in homes, but not usually in homes built since the 1960s. It contains fuses rather than breakers.

Gang. A combining of devices side-by-side, as, a "three-gang" switch box.

GFCI or GFI. A ground-fault circuit interrupter. A device to prevent electrocution, which serves also as a receptacle or (less commonly) as a breaker. I consider the term "ground-fault circuit interrupter" confusing because the word "circuit" is unnecessary and confusing. "Ground fault interrupter" (GFI) clearly states the function it performs – stopping a ground-fault. Since 1973, Code has required GFCI protection for more and more receptacle locations in homes. If connected to properly, a GFCI receptacle is also able to sense and stop ground-faults at any standard receptacles wired on from it. See [31].

Ground. The common reference point for the voltage of a home's electrical system. It refers to an intended or unintended connectedness to the earth. The neutral wires of circuits and of the system are grounded, but a "ground wire" means a separate "grounding" wire keeping metal parts of devices, fixtures, or appliances from becoming electrically hot, and so endangering people or equipment. Installed in homes since the 1960's, these wires are to be either bare or green-covered. The ground wire is not connected so as to be part of the normal path of the circuit, as a neutral is. When a ground wire does carry current, it is supposed to carry so much that it causes the breaker of the circuit to trip, alerting us that a problem needs attention. If things were not grounded, people's bodies would more often be a path for current from a hot wire touching the metal to get to ground – and we do not have enough conductivity to trip a normal breaker!

Ground-fault. Any short circuit finding its path to ground by way of something other than the neutral wire. It is a leaking of current off of the intended path. Most shocks are an example, but more common are faults to grounded metal.

Hot. Or "live." (As an adjective:) Having electrical force (voltage) in relation to ground/earth, especially 120 volts. "Hot" is the termed used because anything even slightly connected to ground (like us!) could get agitated as a path this force uses toward ground. (As a noun:) The wire/terminal/contact that is to be hot, especially the wire from a breaker to lights/appliances.

Hotness. Having voltage in relation to ground, especially 120 volts.

Junction box. As distinguished from any electrical box, a box used only for making connections, not for also connecting to and supporting a switch, receptacle, or light. These other (device or light) boxes often have junctioning going on in them as well, that is, wire-to-wire circuit connections.

Line and Load. These are relative terms. In relation to a given switch or device, "line" refers to wires being "supplied" to it from "upstream," from the direction of the main panel. With regard to the same device, "load" refers to wires or terminals that are "downstream" from or controlled by it. So wires from a switch or GFCI might be load wires with respect to that switch but line wires with respect to another switch downstream from it. Another meaning of "load": a user of electricity; a light or appliance.

Neutral. The wires of a circuit connected ultimately to the power company's earth-related neutral wire. They carry current between there and lights/appliances. Neutrals are always supposed to be white. Contact with them will not normally shock you because they are normally connected to ground much better than you can be.

Open. Unlike an overload or short, an open refers to a circuit no longer being able to carry current because somewhere the path has physically discontinued – by a break, a gap, or a deterioration. In a sense, a switch or breaker breaks the path, but it intends to do so. An open is an unintended discontinuity. Typically, a wire has become too loose at a point where it is supposed to pass current on to another wire.

Outlet. Technically, the point along a circuit where a light or appliance receives its final connections to the hot and neutral of the circuit. In practice, however, we usually mean a receptacle. The following are not outlets: switch, breaker, junction box.

Overload. This is when a circuit has carried a little too much current a little too long, so that the wires will be getting too warm to be safe. The breaker will trip off. You were running a little too much on that circuit. You can now change your habits, plug one of those things into another circuit, let it happen again some other month, or have a new circuit installed for some of those things. So long as breakers do their job, overloading is not dangerous, just inconvenient. Safety people often warn us not to overload outlets or power strips, as if we know how to judge that. The two cases of this so-called overloading that need a little attention are light sockets and extension cords. Just don't exceed their stated wattage or amperage.

Panel. Or "panel box" or "breaker box." The large metal box containing breakers for circuits. The "main" panel or "service" panel would be the central source for the home, receiving its power from the power company. There can be subpanels in a home, fed from the main panel and containing some of the home's circuit breakers. Some people still use the term "fuse box" to refer to a panel, but that term should relate to one having fuses.

Phantom voltage. An inconsequential voltage many testers will detect. It may register as a lower or a full voltage. It seems to come about by means of capacitance or inductance from a nearby hot wire. See [65] and [67].

Pigtail. To provide circuit connection to a fixture, appliance, or device by means of a single wire getting its own connection out of a connector (wire "nut") that contains other wires of the circuit. The other way of connecting would be for incoming and outgoing circuit wires to connect directly to the device's terminals or the fixture's wires. See [93] and an illustration [17].

Receptacle. Or, loosely, "outlet" or "plug" or "plug-in." A receiving device that serves as the outlet for lights or appliances to connect to a circuit by means of a cord with a "plug" on the end.

Short. A short circuit. I am including ground-faults here. A short is basically an unintended continuity from a hot wire to something of different voltage. In a 240-volt circuit, a possible short would involve both hot wires touching (rare). All other shorts in a home will tend to be from a hot to ground by way of a neutral wire, ground wire, or anything providing a conductive path to ground. A short will not trip a breaker if its path has quite a bit of resistance. A short is something other than an overload that can trip a breaker, and for quite a different reason. With a short, the flow of current is not due to the intended limited use of electricity through lights and appliances, but is due to a potentially huge flow of electric power by way of an unintended and (often) very conductive path. Current still flows around in a circuit. But it is a shortcut, so it is called a "short" circuit. An example would be if the hot wire at a light fixture made contact with the metal of the fixture, which, being grounded by a ground wire, sends a lot of current through this path, tripping the breaker.

Socket. Also "lamp holder." The part of a light fixture that receives the bulb or tube. It is understandable that some people use "socket" to mean the receptacles we plug cords into, because in both cases, the one thing is receiving the other thing that actually uses electricity.

Splice. An unanchored electrical connection joining two or more wires. Compare "Terminal."

Submain breaker. One of up to six (double) circuit breakers allowed till 1985 to be the combined means for disconnecting all power to a home's circuits. Since then a single "main breaker" has been the required means. This has provided a confusion, because submains were commonly labeled "Main." When a submain has trouble passing current through one of its points of contact (at its bus bars, its wires, or its internal contacts), it will arc, overheat, possibly trip, and eventually fail to pass current any longer through that half. The result of this is that about half of the 120-volt circuits of the house – those fed by that half – will be dead. See [40].

Switch. A device that purposely interrupts or passes hotness and current to part of a circuit.

Terminal. A screw or other pressure-device to which one or more wires are connected for passing electrical continuity and current along. Like "Splice," but a terminal is anchored in place, often on a device, whereas a splice is free-floating.

Three-way. Although there is a type of light bulb and socket by this name, here we mean a switching system in which a light(s) is controllable from two locations by two switches. The name comes from the usual number of terminals on the switches involved. The term is often used of systems involving more than two switches. See [24].

Travelers. The pair of wires in a three-way switch system that are run (within the same cable) between one switch and the next as the alternate paths for hotness to be passed on.

Voltage. The forcefulness with which electricity is ready to flow. Also, the measurable relation of this force between two points ("volts"). Voltage can be present or fail to be present, and this is not identical with whether current is flowing or not. The relation is this. Current cannot flow if voltage is lacking, but even with voltage available, current will only flow if a continuous and conductive path is provided. Mathematically voltage is the "product" of current (amps) and resistance (ohms), but in practice current is the product, that is, the result, of a provided voltage acting on a given resistance.

Wattage. Rate of electric energy usage by lights or appliances. When applied to devices, it indicates the maximum watts the device is designed to deliver or control (rather than use). Wattage is directly proportional to current and to voltage and is mathematically the product of them (amps times volts). 120 volts driving 15 amps through a resistance means 1800 watts is being used. Roughly equivalent to "volt-amperes."

Wire. A wire is bendable metal for carrying electric current. Except when used as a grounding wire, it is coated with insulating material. In homes, wires that run to outlet and switch locations are mostly within cables. Wire sizes (gauges: "AWG") are (from smallest) 14, 12, 10, 8, 6, 4, etc., with larger wires at the meter and panel using a different numbering system. To understand the function that different wires on a circuit play, see [11]. The functioning of each of these wires is not assured if they are not installed correctly or if they come apart at a connection.

CHAPTER 26

Help From the Author

Larry Dimock
The Circuit Detective

I hope this guide outlives me and is updated by someone as needed. Until it outlives me, it is likely that you will be able to contact me to comment on it or to ask for advice (for a fee) on solving a particular malfunction in your home. One of these might put you in touch with me: (425) 333-4400 or www.thecircuitdetective.com.

Disclaimer

Since we are in a position like a doctor diagnosing and advising a patient remotely, by contacting me you agree that you will not hold me liable in any way for misjudgments, or for any hazards you encounter or produce if you work on your electrical system. Contacting a local electrician to come to your home is always an option and may still be necessary after consulting me.

Made in the USA
Lexington, KY
06 April 2015